Clive Morton qualified as a chartered accountant and immediately joined the Unilever group where he worked in the frozen foods, soap and detergents, and packaging industries in a range of commercial roles. This was followed by general management appointments in the printed packaging, engineering and toy industries before finally starting his own business providing consulting services to the smaller business sector and developing a franchise concept. He now runs an accounting practice with his son.

Opportunities for Redundant Managers

Clive Morton

Constable & Robinson Ltd.
55–56 Russell Square
London WC1B 4HP
www.constablerobinson.com

First published in the UK by How To Books,
an imprint of Constable & Robinson Ltd., 2014

A copy of the British Library Cataloguing in
Publication Data is available from the British Library

ISBN: 978-1-8452-8543-2 (paperback)
ISBN: 978-1-8452-8544-9 (ebook)

Printed and bound in the UK

1 3 5 7 9 10 8 6 4 2

Contents

You Are Not Alone

The world is changing

We live in a fast-changing world where globalisation is having a profound effect and bringing intense competition. The internet, television and modern media have stimulated the appetites and ambitions of the three to four billion people living in the emerging economies, who want the lifestyles that we in the Western world – a population of barely one billion – have enjoyed since we started rebuilding our economies when war ended in 1945. Even before the war, the West enjoyed far higher living standards than elsewhere, though a definite gulf existed between the middle and the lower-income classes. This distinction has become blurred in the late twentieth century but could re-emerge in modern times as salary gaps widen.

Globalisation has brought about significant transfers of Western technology to people who work harder and for longer hours at much lower levels of remuneration. They do not have the social benefits that have provided us with a cushion in times of stress; hence taxes are lower. It is hardly surprising, therefore, that their economies are growing much faster than ours.

Growth in the emerging markets does of course create opportunities for international businesses and those with export ambitions, but it also brings about mergers and acquisitions, with the attendant streamlining and downsizing, as businesses fight for a greater share of world markets. This competitive activity also moves businesses to other locations, where labour costs are cheaper. Indeed, in some cases, entire industries have relocated or been forced out of business. We still have motor manufacturing in the UK, but most of it under foreign ownership. The textile industry, however – a major employer in the north of England in the 1950s – has virtually departed these shores.

Administrative functions like order processing and accounting are increasingly being outsourced. Telesales has virtually become an India-based activity. These trends will continue. The overall effect will be to squeeze labour and administrative incomes, while senior and international managers will experience income growth. There will also be increasing pressure on social benefits, many of which will become unaffordable.

One hundred years ago, Britain still had an empire and was the most prosperous nation on earth. Throughout most of my lifetime, the UK has been one of the top five largest economies in the world, and collectively, Western economies have accounted for well in excess of half the world's gross output. Now the BRIC countries (Brazil, Russia, India and China) account for more than 20 per cent. The UK has slipped to eighth position. I calculate that on current trends, it will contribute only 2 per cent of world output within twenty years, and the whole of Europe will account for barely 10 per cent. Unless we face reality, we could slide into third-world status before the end of this century.

This book is not intended to be a political treatise, but I have briefly sketched the background to show that change in this century will be even more rapid than in the previous one, with a probability of decline in living standards. It is inevitable, therefore, that redundancy will become a common occurrence, quite likely to happen at least once in most careers.

In the following pages, I have discussed how redundant managers in the UK could face up to this problem, set out their options and given practical advice about how to follow through. The underlying philosophy and logic could be applied in any Western country, where the issues are broadly the same, though some institutions and regulations may vary. I have not, therefore, elaborated on compliance requirements, most of which are fully described on the internet. I have also tried to avoid long essays on particular options, as my purpose is more to provoke the imagination and provide outline guidance rather than go into detailed plans. I believe it is also important for the aspiring manager or businessman to bring their own creativity to bear once they have seized upon an idea.

Understanding the impact of redundancy

The immediate effect of redundancy is usually shock, even when it is expected. Like bereavement and divorce, it removes one of the pillars on which you have built your life. It takes time to recover from the trauma and face up to a future that will be different. You will no longer be meeting the colleagues you have been meeting daily for a number of years, or striving to achieve the same objectives.

It is, in many ways, similar to an illness, and should be treated as such. Most people experiencing this unpleasant situation suffer a substantial blow to their pride, a partial loss of identity and, at the very least, an undermining of their confidence – a feeling that they might not be good enough at what they have been doing these last few years.

If it is any comfort, you are not alone in having these feelings. Try not to wallow in self-pity. By all means cosset yourself and treat it as an illness from which you need to recover, but at the same time, try to be positive. There are clichés galore that deal with these dilemmas:

- Every problem is also an opportunity

- Every cloud has a silver lining

- When one door closes another opens

As somebody who has suffered all the above traumas, more than once, I can assure you that these adages are true. Of course life is very different after you have been shown the door, or your spouse dies, but I have come to believe that change is one of the constants, and that life does go on and presents new challenges. I have also grown to believe that life is about confronting problems, and in doing so, finding out about, and facing up to, yourself, because ultimately you are the only person who is able to solve those problems. Luck plays a part, but many people argue that you make your own luck. My own philosophy is that if you are not in the game, there is no chance of being lucky.

Analysing why it happened and moving on

So what do you do? The first thing is to be honest with yourself. Do not be too self-critical or masochistic, but analyse the factors surrounding your dismissal; try to think broadly and laterally.

- Was it due to a personality clash?

- To what extent were you responsible?

- What were the underlying circumstances?

- Was the business in trouble?

- If so, what problems did it face?

- Are they soluble problems or part of long-term decline?

- What is happening in the industry sector?

- Is there a realistic chance you could secure another position within the sector?

- Do you want to?

Progressively you are starting to think about the future. Do you really want to repeat your life over again with a different company? For many people the answer will be yes, and usually for reasons that are important to them, such as responsibility towards their families or the fact that their experience might be valuable to their recent employer's competitors, or that they could secure a better job. Some will have the background and qualifications that enable them to work in different industry sectors and may wish to consider opportunities for employment in a wider field.

Considering self-employment
The alternative, of course, is to consider self-employment. In this case, more options are available. I have considered these under several headings, together with the financial implications and likely investment requirements:

- Advisory services, utilising your own skills and experience

- Product-based businesses

- Acquiring a franchise

- Acquiring an existing business

- Internet-based businesses

Finally I deal with the commercial and legal considerations that are likely to face all businesses sooner or later.

In the short term, there is nothing to prevent you from job-hunting while also researching business opportunities. The worrying factor is that in current conditions, it is taking far longer to find new jobs, so do consider self-employment as a realistic option before you run out of money.

CHAPTER ONE

Exploring Your Aspirations and Capabilities

Facing the situation

Redundancy comes as a shock, but it is likely to be a widely shared experience that obliges most of us to rethink what our lives are about. It can and does occur at any stage, but more usually past the age of forty. This is a particularly hard time for most people, the majority of whom will be married, with children at school and mortgage repayments to meet. This adds pressure to an already difficult situation, as financial commitments and lifestyle changes have to be faced, as well as the overall effect on family and friends. These factors could induce an element of panic.

The first thing to consider, however, is that change is being forced upon you. You therefore need to sit back and ask yourself a series of questions:

- What immediate economies can be effected?

- How long can I survive, assuming I received compensation?

- What is my value in the marketplace?

- Have I been working in a growth or a declining industry?

- What contacts do I have?

- Am I known in the industry?

- What are my chances of finding another job?

- How long is it likely to take?

- Will I have to take a cut in salary?

- Could I work in a different industry sector?

- What other options do I have?

- Am I willing to change locations, schools, etc.?

- Am I willing to work abroad?

- If so, how will the family cope?

- How strong is my marriage?

- What do I want to do with my life?

- What do I want to achieve?

- What are my strengths and weaknesses?

- Would I like to change my life?

- What business ventures would I be good at?

There are other, supplementary questions according to how you answer the primary questions, and it is likely to take a while before you feel the answers in your gut. It may also create further confusion if some of the answers come as a surprise; for example, if you discover that your spouse lacks understanding, is critical of you and not supportive of your ideas, this could lead to a whole new train of thought. But even though you need to take your time answering these questions, don't let that stop you from speaking to industry contacts, firing off a few job applications or looking at business opportunities.

The one thing in your favour is that you now have more time to dwell on issues you have not really been thinking about with any seriousness before. The gut reaction, however, is probably the most important, provided you have faced up to your responsibilities: you cannot realistically go backpacking in Australia, say, if you have children coping with school examinations and developing aspirations of their own.

Certain skills are necessary to carry out management roles, leaving aside technical or product knowledge specific to a particular industry. It could reasonably be assumed that if you have been carrying out a management role for a number of years you have:

- Some organisational ability

- Reasonable communication skills

- Some leadership qualities

- Experience in taking decisions

- Ability to work under pressure and meet deadlines

- Ability to identify and analyse problems

- Experience of working in a team

These are all qualities that set you ahead of Mr or Mrs Average and make you a responsible member of society with a skill set that is of value to the community. They equip you to carry out similar jobs, if available, or give you a head start if you decide that your best option is to start up and build a business of your own.

Most corporate managers are not natural entrepreneurs, however, and unless they have achieved director status, they are likely to lack a comprehensive overview of a business. Having said that, it is important to recognise that people from almost every background and personality type have built successful businesses, so there is nothing stopping experienced managers from doing so, except their own inhibitions.

Thinking clearly

In considering any future possibilities, you need to be clear about your own strengths and weaknesses, talents and limitations, and also about what you really want to achieve. Be honest about your weaknesses. You may well be capable of modifying or controlling them to a degree, but recognise also that some will be a serious disadvantage in particular situations. If, for instance, you are abrasive and do not like meeting strangers, do not think of involving yourself in, say, a retail business, which will bring you into contact with people all day long.

Being positive

Positive thinking and self-belief are essential, coupled with commitment. This implies that you should enjoy what you do and that you are able to set goals for yourself and think through how to achieve them. In doing so, you must anticipate some problems along the way and visualise how to deal with them. But you must keep going forward and trust yourself to achieve.

Being objective

Objectivity is essential, meaning you must think through what your business is about and how far you plan to take it. I will talk more about this later, as it is inevitably tied in with lifestyle and family obligations, but you have to be clear about where you are going and why, and about your personal motivation.

Communication

In most businesses it is desirable to be a fairly good communicator, as indeed it is in most management jobs. It also helps if you like people, as you are likely to be spending time talking to them, finding out about their needs and often persuading them to buy your product or service. There are, of course, businesses that do not involve direct contact with people face to face, such as mail order or trading on the internet, but even here you need to be able to communicate in writing, often in quite a specialised way.

Numeracy

Dealing with numbers is a feature of most businesses, and the majority of managers have some awareness of financial and/or statistical reports. Initially, however, you will need to prepare your own budgets, determine the margins needed and set prices, although in many cases, competition will have determined market prices already.

The important point about the above-listed criteria is that all these qualities can be learned. They are not part of people's nature, therefore nobody is excluded from starting a business on personality or character grounds. It is true that some people handle numbers or communication better than others, but you are not required to graduate in English or mathematics, merely to acquire a reasonable level of competence.

Not all businesses succeed. Sadly, an increasing number fail, particularly in times of recession, but where the initial research has been carried out assiduously and the plan thought through and implemented efficiently, a business can thrive for many years, although it must be prepared to adapt to changing circumstances.

The rewards for success are significant. Most efficient owner-managed businesses generate significantly higher profits than the incomes that could be earned in employment. They bring benefits to the community and usually some employment opportunities for others, as well as personal satisfaction and achievement to the owner, who also has greater freedom and independence.

I know of very few people who have returned to being employed after running a successful business of their own.

The purpose of this book

I do not believe that genuine achievers spend hours reading books on how to do something, or how somebody else has done it. My intention in this book is to set out ideas you need to consider, which you can then tweak according to your own circumstances. If you need more detailed advice after taking the plunge, I will gladly talk to you, and if I cannot help, I will point you in the right direction to obtain the relevant advice. For the most part I am writing about subjects of which I have experience and/or knowledge.

You will find I strongly advocate preparation, information-gathering and planning. I believe in fact-finding, analysing situations, setting out your intentions in writing and keeping goals in sight, but it is also important to remember that circumstances change, so plans must react accordingly. In writing this, I am reminded of a classic case study in which a general manager concluded that his targets were no longer achievable and started grousing to senior management about his business plan and goals. A few days later he received an email from the chief executive: 'Stop thinking about the target and start thinking about how to hit the target.' The plan is not sacrosanct; the goals are.

CHAPTER TWO
Examining Your Employment Options

Finding a new job

Finding a new job is, in most cases, a marketing exercise in which you are the product. You must start by making the product as smart and efficient as it can be to give yourself an edge when you find suitable opportunities. This also means that you need a product specification. The standard form is to produce a curriculum vitae, or CV. This is your most important tool, so consider carefully what it says about you, what it means to the reader and how it compares with the competition.

Jobs that are advertised in national newspapers will receive at least one hundred replies, and sometimes even more than a thousand. The typical recruitment agent is therefore looking for reasons to discard as many applications as possible in order to narrow the search to those who meet the client's requirements most closely. The fee structure is such that they want to interview no more than a dozen people, with a view to submitting a shortlist of four or five candidates with a report on each. They are therefore looking for anything negative – illegible handwriting, too much waffle, no significant achievements, worked for the same company all her life, etc.

Composing your CV
It is immediately obvious that presentation is critical. Your CV should show a career progression, drawing attention to important features, a brief background and contact details. There is no standard format, but I recommend the following example.

CV Jack Smith

Address   **Telephone Number**
                                                         Email

A qualified electrical engineer who has enjoyed a progressive career to technical director in a telecommunications business, with earlier experience in the aeronautics, electronics and computer industries, and who seeks a senior position in a similar field.

Career history (start with most recent appointment)
Period (i.e. 2007–2013)
Final income earned, plus perks
Brief description of business (sector, turnover,
   number of employees)
Your role (responsible for department with 60 staff,
   involved in product design, production and
   organisational matters)
Achievements
(Continue with previous roles in same format)
Education and training (be brief, but include
   qualifications)
Marital status, number of children
**Hobbies, outside interests and any personal
   achievements**

This should run to a maximum of two pages, neatly typed or printed and ideally retained on your computer so that you are able to modify it to highlight points that coincide with the prospective employer's stated requirements (e.g. you might mention different achievements in previous occupations). Its purpose is to gain you an interview, and the format will help an interviewer to obtain a general impression and direct him to raise questions that you should be able to answer to show yourself in the best light.

Networking your friends

Your network of friends and industry contacts is a good place to start, because you have the immediate advantage of being known to them. You can use them to evolve a more polished approach and learn from the questions they ask, so that you are better prepared when confronted with a potential employer. Essentially you are enquiring if they know of any openings or opportunities they could refer you to or, better still, recommend you for. At the very least you want them to put you in touch with other contacts that could be helpful. This may require you to swallow a certain amount of pride, but networking is one of the best methods for finding new opportunities.

You could consider LinkedIn and Facebook. There are some risks with this, as you could attract emails from time-wasters, but social networking can be a useful tool nevertheless.

Approaching head-hunters and recruitment agencies

Head-hunters are rarely engaged to find people below board level and have relatively few clients. They receive many direct approaches, but even so, it is well worth sending a CV with a short covering letter enquiring if they could put you forward for positions they are aware of. Some of the more enterprising head-hunters create opportunities for themselves by writing to chief executives along the lines: 'I have a particular candidate whom I believe could be useful to your organisation ...'

Letters to management recruitment agents should be personally addressed and targeted at those who appear to be working in industry sectors that are of interest to you. They are generally less effective than head-hunters, as they are overwhelmed with applications and are therefore likely to ignore you unless you are a potential fit for a position they are currently dealing with.

Contacting prospective employers

A further approach is to write directly to chief executives in your industry sector and allied fields, enclosing your CV. It helps if you can tie the approach in with some news event: e.g. 'I was interested to read about your expansion plans in the Financial Times recently and thought this might create employment opportunities ...' This will probably be passed down the line to the head of HR or the expansion programme, but should elicit some reply and possibly an invitation to meet.

Applying for advertised positions

Senior management appointments usually appear in the Sunday Times or Telegraph, but you should also skim trade journals and local newspapers. Some advertisers still use box numbers to collect replies, but many display the company name. Where this happens, you should scour the internet for information about the company so that you are reasonably informed. You should also consider the wording of the advert carefully. Most describe the job and the person they are looking for. Your objective is therefore to match such criteria as closely as possible. Again your response should include a CV with a covering note that draws attention to the way in which you match requirements.

Attracting attention

Your objective with the above campaign is to obtain an interview as a precursor to being offered a new appointment. You should therefore try to visualise the impact of your correspondence on its recipient. Most professional recruiters receive hundreds of letters daily. The sheer volume is a major reason why employers delegate recruitment to agents. This means you are already in a competitive situation, and thus something about you has to stand out. Clearly your CV should be freshly printed and not creased, so send it in an A4 envelope. Your covering letter should be concise, a maximum of four paragraphs, and should *never* run to a second page. It should relate closely to the advertisement and show a connection. If you are making an unsolicited approach, indicate that you know something about the company. Below are a couple of examples to help those of you who have little experience of making job applications.

Dear Sirs (use a name if given in the advertisement)

Technical Director – Electronics Industry

Please consider me for the above position recently advertised in the *Sunday Times*. My CV is enclosed.

I am a qualified electrical engineer with twenty-two years' experience in the industry. My most recent appointment was as technical director with the XYZ Company, where I reorganised the production flow to achieve substantial economies and increase output.

I was made redundant following the acquisition of XYZ by the ABC Group and now seek a new appointment. I believe I closely match the criteria you are seeking and would welcome an opportunity to discuss this further at an interview.

Yours etc.

A letter to a chief executive:

Dear Mr Cameron

Congratulations on your recent results and your record of ongoing growth within the electronics industry.

I have over twenty years' experience in production and design, most recently as technical director of the XYZ Company, where I reorganised production to achieve economies and increase output. Following the acquisition of this company by the ABC Group, I was made redundant and seek a new position.

My CV is enclosed. I would greatly appreciate a meeting to explore mutually whether you have any suitable opportunities within your group.

Yours etc.

I offer these examples as a suggestion as to how you should consider responding to advertisements or approaching major personalities within your industry sector. You should, at all times, use your own style. My second letter flatters slightly without being too deferential and indicates some awareness of the CEO's business and progress.

Preparing for the interview

If you are invited for an interview, you should dress smartly though not be overdressed. It is foolish to put yourself at a disadvantage or try to be the oddball. One or two creative professions, like artists or software designers, accept casual clothing, but most managers and directors are expected to look and be smart. Management recruitment agents and head-hunters are probably aiming to prepare a shortlist of candidates to put before their clients, so when meeting them, your objective is to make it on to that list.

Most professionals will try to put you at ease with a pre-liminary conversation. Try to relax, breathe deeply and do not tense up.

- Look directly at the interviewer and maintain good eye contact

- Be honest; do not exaggerate

- Do not waffle; get to the nub of the questions

- Some elaboration to set things in context is acceptable

- Show enthusiasm and ask questions about the business and the position on offer

- Comment on how your experience fits with the position

Where the prospective employing company is known before you attend the interview, you should carry out research about the business and let it emerge during the conversation that you have done some homework. Do not be timid or too pushy, but try to ensure your strengths have been brought out during the interview process. Make sure you allude to them, or even use the odd anecdote to show the relevance of your experience. Treat it as a two-way conversation, not an interrogation.

If you conclude that the position under discussion is not one you would want, do not hesitate to say so. The interviewer may have other clients, and if you earn his respect, you could ask about them.

Considering self-employment
A different way of life

Self-employment is an option that takes a certain amount of courage and significant changes in lifestyle and mental attitude. In today's world, however, it is something that needs to be seriously considered. I have met many people of fifty-plus, and even younger, who, having lost their job and tried for a while to find a new one, have given up completely. Some of them have never truly worked again.

What a waste!

Life is a constant challenge. I believe that if you have never been down, you will never appreciate being up. Nature is in a constant state of change. Human beings cannot avoid it. I would encourage anybody whose spirits are low after redundancy and recognize that it is going to be hard to find a new job, to strike out on their own. Make a new life and become self-reliant and independent.

Success brings its own rewards. As a flourishing business owner you can expect to achieve higher income than you received in employment. You will be respected within your peer group and have the confidence that comes from knowing that your success is down to your own efforts.

Understanding the realities of self-employment
Self-employment is not for the work-shy. The probability,

at least in the early stages, is that you will work longer hours than you did when you were in employment. You are, however, your own boss and do not have to try to anticipate how somebody else will view your efforts or worry that they will hold you to account. You need to think through situations that confront you, decide a course of action and get on with it. You do not need to hold meetings with colleagues, so your time is used more productively.

Most importantly, you are in control. Things can still go wrong and you have to put them right or plan around them, but you are always in a position to take action. I remember when I started out, my very first client meeting was cancelled. It seemed enormously frustrating at the time, but now I simply make another appointment and carry on with something else. A client dropping out altogether is, of course, a bigger problem, but if you are working effectively, something or somebody usually takes their place within a reasonable time frame.

You have to plan your time carefully, and there are administrative functions or other chores that you will come to hate doing. That's life, however, and if the business succeeds, such chores can be delegated. The major advantage, of course, is that the profits belong to you. (It will not be long before the man from the Inland Revenue arrives with a shovel to help himself, but more about that later.)

Benefiting the community

Starting a business is also advantageous to the community at large. I often feel that in this country we do not give enough credit or recognition to the people who do start out on their own, with all the attendant risks. In doing so, they become part of the real economy, which is the only true source of income from which the community is able to benefit, and the only provider of genuine employment. This is often forgotten in our overtaxed land, where faceless bureaucrats try to dictate how we should behave, overlooking the fact that without soundly based commercial activity, there would be no taxation base out of which their salaries could be paid.

CHAPTER THREE

Choosing a Product- or Service-Based Business

If you decide that working for someone else is no longer for you, and want to start your own business, you will need to decide whether you are going to offer a product or a service. This is a serious preliminary consideration, because few managers have genuine experience of trading unless they have a background in sales and/or marketing, and even then, many lack the buying experience. (I am ruling out manufacturing as an opportunity for all but a very few. I will discuss this later, but the investment required to set up an operating plant is likely to be large, the project will be time-consuming and there are certain to be technical problems that people starting up a business could do without. The other feature of this position is that most UK manufacturing companies have excess production capacity, so it is relatively easy for them to subcontract production, saving investment cost and set-up time.)

Some services are, of course, packaged as products, such as a haircut or a shave, usually offered at a price. Others might emerge as a finished product, such as tailoring where you buy a bespoke suit. The essential point is that you must choose between offering a service that you arrange or carry out yourself, and dealing in products that you buy and sell. The latter is likely to involve higher cash investment and is therefore a greater risk.

Choosing a product-based business

If you choose products, you have the option of distributing through:

- Retail

- Direct

- Mail order

- Internet

- Party plan or network marketing

- Sales agency

If you can visualise yourself running any of the above types of business, let's go on to examine the differences between them.

Becoming a retailer

Although being a grocer or a newsagent is quite different from dealing in antiques or selling fishing tackle, in principle you are all doing the same thing: using a window to summon passers-by into your shop, although with fishing tackle and antiques, buyers are more likely to actively seek you out, because their requirements are specialist and/or specific.

If you are considering becoming a retailer, I recommend being a specialist. Property costs are high, particularly for primary sites, and the supermarkets are selling wider ranges of products and undercutting the high street retailers. Home shopping through catalogues, mail order and the internet is diverting sales from retail. This two-way squeeze is driving traditional retailers out of business.

Specialist shops do not usually need primary sites. Many such establishments now have websites and promote themselves through the internet. (The internet has become an important marketing tool, so I will deal with this specifically in the chapter about marketing.) They also attend trade fairs, and build lists of clients to whom they offer specific products as they become available. These types of dealers are not waiting for people to come through the door, but are actively promoting their businesses.

Money can still be made with sporting goods, hobbies and other specialities. Butchers and bakers continue to do well, but usually through seeking a wider audience by supplying caterers, pubs and restaurants, or selling sandwiches from vans on industrial estates.

Direct selling

Selling to the general public door-to-door evokes memories of the old commercial travellers, or even tinkers in earlier times. A few franchise concepts still exist where products have to be demonstrated, but this is more in the field of party plan and/or network marketing. The sole trader who sells to industry is usually an agent. This can be lucrative, although sometimes cyclical.

Some UK firms take on agents who operate within a given territory and earn commission, but this is almost tantamount to employment. The more usual arrangement is to act as British agent for an overseas manufacturer. Typically you would be selling machinery, computers or software, and occasionally components. It would rarely apply to perishable goods, where specialist warehousing and immediate distribution would be necessary, again needing substantial investment.

Most principals expect their agents to hold stock or demonstration models or to have a showroom, so some outlay is necessary, but commission is typically 15 per cent plus. To be truly successful you ideally need a range of loosely allied products: e.g. if you sell bottle-filling machinery, it would be sensible to deal in capping and labelling equipment too. In this way you are potentially selling a production line rather than just one machine.

Selling through mail order

This is a growth industry, as people are increasingly buying through catalogues or special promotions. There is some complexity in handling a range of products, however, particularly with items like clothing, where it is necessary to stock a range of sizes and provide a choice of colours and designs. You might well be offering in excess of a hundred items, which sell in different proportions to each other.

With a few products only, it is possible to run a successful one-person business by subcontracting the handling of orders to a fulfilment house. Specialist businesses will also provide a service of stuffing sales letters into envelopes and arranging postage. One or two printers provide an insertion and postage service.

If you are contemplating this sort of business, it is probably wise to start with a single product and gradually put together a range of items that all sell to the same market. You might start with slimming tablets that cost less than £50 for a six-week trial and generate repeat orders. The next stage might be to add a simple exercise product at less than £100, followed by an advanced machine at under £500. Once you have established credibility and trust, you will find that customers like to deal with you, and repeat purchases help to build your business profitably. In reality, you do not need a vast customer list.

There are great opportunities in combining internet marketing and mail order; I will be describing how to develop this type of business much more fully in Chapter Five (see p.43).

Building a sales agency

Sales agency is a business arrangement whereby you obtain the rights to sell somebody else's product(s), usually within a defined territory, e.g. you become the British agent for a German product, or the Yorkshire agent for a UK product.

The nature of the available products varies significantly, from repeat-purchase consumable products to expensive equipment. It is implicit in the arrangement that you will be required to carry out most of the personal selling to identified customers. In many cases you will need to hold stock; in others you will be expected to have demonstration machines or to take potential customers to the manufacturer's premises or to international exhibitions.

Commission rates range from say 5 per cent for consumable products to in excess of 15 per cent for technical equipment. Opportunities are hard to find and you may need to carry out wide-ranging research, but quite large businesses have been built using this formula, particularly if, as part of the process, you are able to accept older machinery in part exchange and find a market for reconditioned equipment.

Selling through party plan and network marketing

These practices are used by companies who produce products for the general public that need some form of demonstration. A word of caution, however: network marketing in particular is sometimes closely linked to pyramid selling, in which people at the top make fast money at the expense of those at the bottom.

Party plan evolved more as a part-time, social business in which agents invite friends and contacts to their homes or meeting places to show off the products and induce guests to purchase something, on which they then earn commission. This can work well for a while but needs a constant flow of new products to maintain interest.

In network marketing, somebody is induced to buy a product for their own use and then purchase several more to sell to their friends, thus joining the network. You also gain a commission on all sales made by members of your network. It can be a clever manner in which to carry out a test market for the original producer, but since very few products have a long life, it is necessary to acquire new products at regular intervals if you wish to make a career of this. Some people are successful in the early stages, but by its nature, network marketing has a high failure rate, and as such is not a business I intend spending much time on.

Choosing a service-based business

Many services, such as dry-cleaning, hairdressing, shoe repairs, etc., are, of course, provided through retail premises. A fundamental difference between products and services, however, is that in providing services, you are effectively selling time. Charges are usually offered at hourly or daily rates, or calculated with reference to how long it takes to cut somebody's hair, for example. There is a limit to what can be achieved. You can, of course, gear up and employ other people, but their capacity is also limited by time. A salesman could sell ten products to one customer and a hundred to another in the same amount of time.

The potential with products is far greater than with services, but so too is the risk. While you can never be sure how many products you can sell, once your service-based business is established, you can be more certain about time. There is, though, a risk related to your health and fitness. Your product can still sell despite illness, but you cannot usually provide a service if you are ill for any length of time. However, this is an insurable risk.

Providing professional services

The original professions – medicine, teaching, law and architecture – are long established. Other professions have grown in support of business – accountancy, property surveying and management, finance and insurance, marketing and advertising – and people with these skills could seriously consider setting themselves up in their chosen field.

There are, of course, differences between how the various professions are managed and the nature of the business. Traditionally clients have always visited lawyers, doctors and accountants, although audits are usually carried out on clients' premises and doctors do go out to patients who are too ill to visit them. Many doctors and accountants practise from their own homes; lawyers less so. Architects and surveyors need to visit clients' premises, but many use their homes as trading addresses.

Selling life assurance and investment plans to the general public usually entails visiting prospective clients in their own homes, often during the evening, to explain what it is all about and to advise on available options. Many life assurance brokers are tied to a particular company. Risk insurance brokers read the market on behalf of clients to arrange the most appropriate cover. They usually operate from offices or retail premises, where clients visit them.

Advertising agencies need to have access to a range of skills, though not necessarily under one roof. People such as graphic designers and copywriters set up individual businesses that are tantamount to professional practices, and many of these view advertising agencies as potential clients.

Providing wider management services

This is a growing opportunity area that has the potential to become a profession in its own right. Management consultancy first appeared before the Second World War and has become firmly established, although it is probably more vulnerable to fluctuations within the economy than other professions.

It has also become fashionable for redundant managers to carry out projects while job-hunting and to call themselves consultants. I shall be strongly advocating this as a serious career opportunity, similar in many ways to existing professions. It has a low cost of entry into business and should provide a rewarding career, particularly to redundant managers. Consultancy needs a changed mindset, in that you have to capture assignments. This necessitates meeting clients, usually on their premises, and suggesting ways in which you might help to improve their business on a temporary or project basis.

The manner in which you can achieve this is set out fully in the section on marketing (see p.88). I strongly believe that managers from a wide range of backgrounds can apply their skills in this manner. This includes personnel managers, management accountants, IT specialists, quality controllers, buyers and marketing managers.

Service businesses are easy to start and have the advantage of requiring your skills and experience. In most cases, within two years you should be able to establish a business that provides significantly higher income than you earned as an employee in a similar field.

Acquiring a business

Buying an existing business is an option that will require investment. There are some low-cost franchises available, such as carpet cleaning or home motor-repairs, but generally speaking you are likely to need well in excess of £50,000 by the time you have factored in working capital, purchase price and the inevitable learning curve. With established businesses or well-respected franchises, it is usually possible to borrow half this cost from a bank – and sometimes more.

The advantage of buying an established business – subject to due diligence and careful investigation – is that you are usually able to generate immediate income, and if you have done your homework carefully, you can also build the business further.

Franchises are slightly different, in that you are usually starting a new business within a given area and are required to follow the existing business model. Sound franchisors will provide introductory training and marketing support.

I have devoted the next chapter to explaining this subject more fully.

An overview

There are numerous options for self-employment, but for the purposes of this book, I am focusing on **products, services** and **acquisitions**. In the following chapters I will be presenting various aspects of starting, running and building a business, and discussing the differences that apply with these types of businesses.

Let me say immediately that I fully appreciate that the training of an architect is quite different to that of a quality-control manager. It is for you to understand the nature of your own trade or profession. What I am talking about are the marketing, accounting and financial practices that can be applied in any situation and combined with your specific technical skills in order to build a successful business and a satisfying career.

CHAPTER FOUR
Buying a Business

Buying a business is a possible avenue for any former manager who finds himself redundant and seeking a new opportunity. Acquiring an existing business has some obvious advantages, in that a major part of the initial risk can be avoided and you start with an immediate income. There are some problems, however. Good businesses are hard to find and are not usually available unless the owner is dead, ill or about to retire. You have to be sure what you are getting, and there may be some difficulty in valuing the business and reaching agreement about the price and precisely what it includes.

Carrying out due diligence

The process of due diligence ensures that you obtain all the facts about the business you are buying before signing contracts. In most situations the vendor will acknowledge that you need to carry out an investigation and will usually co-operate. If he says, 'That's the price. Take it or leave it,' walk away fast. This might turn out to be one of the most important decisions of your lifetime, so you need to be confident that you will receive what you pay for. If the business is a significant size, with property involved, you should probably retain a lawyer, and if you do not really understand balance sheets and accounts, employ an accountant.

You should set out your questions under the following headings:

Trade
Examine the accounts of each of the last 3–5 years. Ideally you want to see:

- Rising trends in sales, profits and margins
- Schedule of assets used in the business
- Bank borrowings, if any, and how they are secured
- Amount of working capital tied up in the business – debtors and stocks less creditors
- Terms of trade
- List of overdue debtors

Property
- Is it freehold or leasehold?
- Terms of lease, if applicable; how many years to run?
- Is there an area plan of buildings?
- Expansion possibility
- Parking area and access
- Condition of building
- Insurance cover

- Any restrictions
- Local council plans that could change the nature of the location

The market

- How is it defined – by geography, product, etc.?
- Any special features, e.g. licences, etc.
- Main competitors
- Major customers
- How are products/services sold?

Management

- Is the owner so closely involved that the business would be damaged without him?
- Who are the other key players? Examine their contracts and meet them
- How is the business structured?
- How many employees?
- Any trade unions involved?

Goodwill

- Does it exist?
- Does the company have a reputation for anything in particular?

- Any specific expansion possibilities?

- Any serious threats?

- Are staff relations good?

Valuation

- Comparison of market value of assets compared with balance-sheet values

- Add net working capital

- What percentage of total assets do profits represent (return on capital)?

- How does the price asked relate to asset valuations?

- How is any difference explained?

The answers to the above questions will, of course, give rise to further questions. Generally speaking, it would be unwise to pay more than three times net profits of the business, after management salaries, unless:

- The asset values are significantly more than this sum

- The trend in sales and profits is rising fast

- You are confident you can build the company into something substantially more

If you start with this guideline, you have a clear objective.

Conducting negotiations

The above process should have given you some indication of the price you want to pay. If this is miles away from what the owner is asking, you may not be able to reach agreement, so be prepared to walk away.

In any case, after due reflection, you should list the positives and negatives about the business and take them to the meeting as an aide-memoire. Thereafter, it is a question of style as to how you proceed. Personally I like to go straight to the heart of the matter by using a lot of questions.

Q   'How much are you asking?'
A   'A hundred thousand.'
Q   'And how did you reach that valuation?'
A   'That's what my accountant advises.'
Q   'On what basis? The lease has only three years to run and the rent can only be adjusted upwards. And we have already agreed that most of the equipment will need replacing within three to five years.'
A   'Hmm. I need a hundred grand.'
Q   'I would like to help you. But what do you think the bank will say when I tell them I need a hundred thousand pounds to buy a business that makes fifteen thousand a year before tax?' Pause before continuing. 'The cheapest rate I can borrow at is twelve per cent. You know banks. They'll want an arrangement fee up front of at least a thousand.'

The questions are intended to implant the message that the price does not make commercial sense, and hopefully to start a rational discussion about the true market value.

It may be that the vendor will not budge, but you can leave an offer on the table while pursuing other options and speak on the telephone periodically. At the end of the day you really cannot afford to offer a price that doesn't make sense.

Buying a franchise

The concept of franchising has been around since before the Second World War, and if properly structured, it has advantages to both franchisor and franchisee.

Franchising is a means of quickly establishing a national presence for a new business concept or product, at the same time raising expansion capital from the franchisees, who are effectively running their own business within a form of group or partnership structure under contractual arrangements. It follows that both parties need to make an adequate return on their investment and effort.

In practical terms, the franchisor has created either a product or a system that is being licensed to the franchisee. The former would expect to provide training and support in return for an initial fee and investment and ongoing royalties and service charges. The franchisor is granting a territory for the franchisee to exploit, usually by guaranteeing not to open a similar franchise within a given radius or postal code.

The advantage to the franchisee is that he is buying a proven business model or product, so that by following the system, he can achieve a sales and profit expectation. His expansion opportunities are limited by the territory, but with many concepts it is possible to acquire more than one franchise, and this is often encouraged. Expansion is ultimately capped, but risk is lowered, which is why I call it a halfway house. Technically you have a business and the franchisor is not your boss, although you must abide by the rules as set out in the contract and, of course, settle the royalties and service charges monthly.

Typical franchise operations

The British Franchise Association (BFA) lists a few hundred members, all of whom have been vetted by the association to ensure that a proper business model has been set up and proved to be profitable, that the contracts are basically fair to franchisees, and that they will obtain reasonable value for their initial investment.

Initial fees should cover provision of an operating manual, practical training in the business system, and help in finding appropriate premises and raising finance, if applicable. Opportunities range from setting up a mobile carpet cleaning business at probably less than £10,000 to opening a Holiday Inn at possibly several million.

Many restaurant chains have adopted this concept – Pizza Express, Domino's Pizza and Pizza Hut are fairly typical examples. They all offer a range of menus at reasonable prices and, quite often, a takeaway service. Domino's guarantees to deliver telephone orders within half an hour. Kentucky Fried Chicken is probably the most successful franchise business of all; it claims that several franchisees have become millionaires, usually by running a group of outlets.

Dynarod, a long-established business providing a drain clearance service, is another successful business, and some franchises now change hands at in excess of £1 million. Printing shops providing a local service aimed at both the public and small businesses are nearly all franchises. They probably cost in the order of £100,000 to establish, but many generate a six-figure income for successful franchisees.

Professional services have also been franchised. I started a business many years ago providing strategic consultancy services to smaller businesses – planning, marketing and systems – with associates operating on a regional basis. Other companies have sprung up providing completion of tax returns, will-writing services, auditing of bank and credit card charges and other niche services. They are usually able to undercut local accountants and solicitors with a stereotyped product. I can visualise other business services that could be marketed in similar fashion today.

The model franchise

Ideally a franchise business should start with a fully developed prototype or model that can be used to write up an operating manual describing how the business operates. This can then be replicated throughout the country, achieving similar results in every area. It cannot be written into the contract as a guarantee, but the probability should be that if you follow the system, you should be capable of generating an income similar to that of the model.

Carry out your own due diligence

If you are contemplating buying a franchise, you should examine the model, talk to the franchisee in charge, and visit other franchisees to ensure you obtain a rounded picture of how it operates in practice and what support you can rely on. The contract should be clear and simple, setting out the franchisor's and franchisee's obligations and the commercial terms comprehensively.

Much will depend on the nature of the business. With retail or restaurant businesses, the location may well be paramount and it will be equally important to ensure that you are paying a similar rental to that quoted in the model. You can reasonably expect to receive help from the franchisor in both finding a property and negotiating the terms.

Remember, the franchisor needs you to be successful and does not want to be saddled with a failed branch that might damage the reputation of the business as a whole.

Borrowing to finance a franchise

Where significant investment is involved, you are likely to need to borrow. Again, you should expect the franchisor to assist in negotiations with your bank and to present a comprehensive account of the performance and achievements of other franchisees and the level of solvency of the main company. They should also help you prepare, or at least vet, your business plan. Other franchisees may be customers at the same bank, so much of the information you present can be easily verified.

CHAPTER FIVE
Finding Products

In considering likely options for starting a business, I ruled out manufacturing because of the high capital cost and the very high risk. I also asserted that excess production capacity exists within the UK and that subcontracting production would be a better way to go. Indeed, you could even seek production in China, the Philippines or Africa.

I also eliminated wholesaling as a likely business start-up, although you could acquire a wholesaling business. The reality is that if you are going to deal with products, you are essentially a trader.

Finding products to market and distribute

You could create your own product, but it is more probable that you will source something you believe will sell. This might be achieved by asking a manufacturer to produce to your design, or by acquiring the rights under a licence agreement. The possible range is immense. You might be interested in fashion products such as swimwear or multi-coloured silk scarves, sporting equipment, indoor games or toys, electrical components, furniture, oriental rugs, etc.

Likely commodities can be found by visiting international trade fairs or searching the internet. If dealing internationally, you will probably have to buy in bulk, which means cash up front, and take delivery into some form of warehouse. This could be leased, but you will need staff to handle the merchandise, maintain stock records and arrange physical delivery to customers or outlets. In the short term, you could utilise the services of a fulfilment house, provided you are handling non-perishable, smaller products that can be sent by post. I will describe this service more fully below.

Once you have created or sourced a product, or range, the ongoing business activity is primarily about marketing. This type of business takes time and entrepreneurial flair to pull everything together. Depending on the nature of the product, it will also require investment in stock and working capital. You are unlikely to obtain much credit from suppliers, particularly if importing. The business can be run from home, a rented office or a warehouse.

Planning the business

I will deal with finance in a later chapter, and also more fully with marketing, but certain features need to be thought through in the initial stages of almost every business. You will need to cover the following ground:

- Negotiate a contract, subject to evaluation of the market (this is similar to agreeing to buy a house subject to survey)

- Try to assess what similar products are available in the market, and at what range of prices

- How are competing products being sold?

- Try to evaluate the total market; what is the growth potential?

- Consider a test market before becoming fully committed

- Assess the capital requirements based on – say – a container load per month

- Seek premises

- Determine a selling price and calculate margins

- Prepare a budget for operating costs, i.e. rent, rates, heat and light, staff salaries, telephones, etc.

- Prepare a marketing budget – advertising, internet promotion, promotional literature, PR, sales commissions, etc.

- Calculate how many products you need to sell to cover these costs

As you can see, this is quite a large undertaking, with several factors to investigate before you can determine viability. The complexity perhaps underscores my earlier comments that products need significantly more investment than service businesses. The risk is greater and so is the potential reward.

This type of business is not for everybody – probably only those who reached director level in their previous careers and have experience of marketing and finance. As such, it might be ideal for two people with complementary skills to run as a partnership, but almost certainly within a limited company. It is a full general management role that requires flair, good communication skills and close monitoring of a range of activities. If successful, you would soon need to engage staff to operate effectively and maintain growth.

This is the type of trading activity that could be turned into a large business, capable of generating high income while building capital value. Less ambitious people could, of course, run smaller-scale operations.

Running a retail business

The nature of retailing has changed dramatically over a generation. There was a time when it provided a good living. Indeed, when I was a boy growing up in a small town, virtually every shop was privately managed. Many retailers owned the property and lived above the shop.

Walk through any country town today and you will notice that most outlets are part of a group, providing merchandise identical to its associates in other towns. You might also notice that a number of charity shops have taken over the premises of failed businesses. The privately owned concerns are probably hanging on by their fingernails.

The profits are in property

Rentals have to a large extent killed small retailers. Property owners much prefer longer leases with multiple retailers, who offer a better covenant. This helps the owner or developer to raise a larger mortgage and thereby expand his own businesses, secure in the knowledge that he has viable long-term tenants.

Rates, calculated by most councils as a percentage of rents, are periodically assessed and then subjected to annual inflationary increases. These two charges come ahead of everything else. Rent is usually charged up front; rates can be spread over ten months. Credit is not allowed. It is not uncommon to find rent and rates exceeding 15 per cent of turnover. For businesses such as grocers, newsagents and tobacconists, where gross margins are only in the range of 30–35 per cent, this is a swingeing expense. Where margins are higher, volume is usually lower.

Some retailers do make money

Retail was once viewed as a reactive business where you waited for buyers to come into the shop. This is no longer the case. Very few retailers are able to survive on shop takings alone and have needed to become more proactive and develop other lines of business. I have already mentioned butchers and bakers. Some fishmongers do a cold-calling delivery service; pubs try to rustle up more business with steak evenings, summer barbecues and music nights.

Using the internet

Specialist retailers are increasingly creating interactive websites where browsers are able to raise queries about particular requirements and products can be advertised. An important tactic is also to gather the names and contact addresses of browsers who express an interest and to send periodic messages and sales blurbs, as well as interacting with blogs and short articles. This is a low-cost form of advertising that helps keep people aware of you. If you have products that collectors are interested in, it is an effective way of promoting them.

Footfall

For most retailers, location is of vital importance. Before committing to particular premises, you should do periodic counts of the number of people who pass the shop window at various times of the day, and compare this with other locations. All you need is a notepad in which to record a tick for everybody passing by over a half-hour period. This will give a quick impression of how busy the area is compared with other parts of town.

Choose products with care

We have already seen that many retailers fail. This can be attributed to rents that are too high, margins that are too low and inadequate volume due to being in the wrong location. Unless you have something special to offer, it is almost a given that you should not compete with multiple retailers operating in the same town. They will almost certainly have chosen the best location and their buying power is greater than yours. The same applies to products sold through supermarkets. I am not going to try to list products that might succeed, because management and creativity are also part of the mix. How you display merchandise will have a bearing on sales, as will the first impression customers form when they come into the shop.

You have to be different and you must promote strongly.

A business in decline

Homeowners and the general public are still spending broadly the same amount of money on essential products and luxuries, but increasingly in a different manner. Home shopping, whether through catalogues, mailshots or the internet, has become popular and has seen consistently high growth in recent years. This has squeezed the traditional retailers operating from town-centre shops.

Services sold through retail premises are still succeeding, but few openings are available for new businesses unless they are part of a total sales package that includes mail order and/or trade fairs. As a general statement, the volume of business through traditional retail outlets is in progressive decline.

Creating a mail-order business

By setting up your own mail-order business, you are entering an expanding market with excellent opportunities. The speed with which you can build this type of business, however, might depend on the resources you have available and the products you choose. Ideally you should start with a single product and quickly add a more expensive one aimed at the same market, followed by a third, luxury-type item.

In choosing your products you need to think about how they will be distributed and the costs of distribution. This is why I favour handling smaller items that can be sent through the post – books, CDs, health goods, training programmes, etc.

Fulfilment houses

With smaller products, sent by post, you are able to use the services of a fulfilment house. These businesses hold stock, receive orders on your behalf, bank cheques, arrange delivery and send you a full accounting at agreed intervals. Clearly you must use their address in your literature for receipt of orders. Charges are relatively modest, usually comprising a monthly admin charge plus a handling, postage and packing charge per item. Often the post and packing is added to the price of the product, so that the service is almost free – or, more correctly, included.

List brokers

List brokers specialise in building lists of people who have bought various products through mail order, usually over the last two years. Such lists are categorised and might be arranged by age, income or type of product purchased. They are made available to mail-order companies on a rental basis, but may only be used once.

Test marketing

With most new products it pays to carry out a trial run in which you rent a list of, say, 1,000 names of people who have bought similar products. You then produce a sales letter and send it to the potential customers identified. Unless you are particularly good at writing advertising copy, I strongly recommend you use the services of a professional copywriter. The list and the letter are critical to your success. You have to motivate people to buy.

Measuring the response

In planning the test market, you should calculate a budget that shows your costs for a range of mailings – say 1,000, 3,000, 5,000 and 10,000. Printers prefer longer runs and this lowers the cost per letter. You may find the total costs are, say, £2,000, £3,500, £4,500 and £6,000 respectively, bringing the cost per mailshot down from £2 per unit at a 1,000 mailing to 60p per shot if mailing 10,000.

Assume that your gross margin is £75 per unit sold and you obtain a response of 1.2 per cent. This means you sell 12 items to a list of 1,000 names at £75 each, earning £900. You appear to have lost £1,100 on the test run. On the other hand, if you achieved the same result with a mailing to 10,000 names, you would receive 120 orders at £75 each, or

£9,000, showing a profit of £3,000. This implies you would break even with a 5,000 mailing.

In these circumstances you have a slightly difficult decision to take. Should you commit £6,000 and go for 10,000 letters?

Having a follow-through product

In this situation it would be helpful to have a second, more valuable product in stock. This would allow you to include a letter about the additional product when dispatching to customers who have ordered the initial product.

The gross margin on the second product might be £120 per unit. Supposing 20 per cent of the existing customers bought this product. This would earn you a further £240 on the test market. If the same result was achieved with a mailing of 5,000, you would earn a further £1,440, making it a profitable venture. You could then confidently proceed with a 10,000 mailing, or even a larger one.

Assessing gross margins

Much depends on how you perceive the market price in this business. If you are selling products where this, or the price of similar products, is known, you can quickly determine the price you have to pay and work out the margin. Established businesses with catalogues or a range of products seek a minimum gross margin of 80 per cent, or five times product cost, and with some products, ten times product cost. Clearly you cannot afford to be shy about prices. Ideally you want to be selling low-cost products at the highest prices possible.

Returns on mailshots and adverts are relatively low. This is affected by price, quality of sales letter and reputation of the vendor. The returns when selling from a catalogue that offers a substantial range of products would be substantially higher. This type of business is much more complex, however.

Keeping statistics
In a mail-order business, you need to be evaluating virtually everything you do.

- Measure the returns on every mailshot

- Check the number of rejects and underlying reasons

- Compare the extent to which add-ons increase sales, e.g. 3 for the price of 2

- Analyse returns, where possible, by geography, age and income

- Check response from adverts in various journals and newspapers by using codes

Always measure the profitability of each operation. The objective is to optimise your marketing activity.

Starting a sales agency
Salesmen are usually thought of as extroverts, and yet the majority spend a considerable amount of time on their own, driving from one meeting to the next, usually thinking about how they will handle it. They are, perhaps, more conscious of the competitive situation they face than most of their office-bound colleagues, and hence more commercially aware. Psychologically they are closely in tune with self-employed business operators. It is not, therefore, a large

step to take the next move and set themselves up in business. What they first need to decide is whether their interest lies in organising sales or in meeting customers face to face to negotiate deals.

For those who like the cut and thrust of meeting people and doing deals, becoming a self-employed salesman earning commission is an obvious way forward. It does, however, require close analysis of both markets and products. As always, the starting point is a consideration of your own background and industry knowledge. What and who do you know? What type of products have you handled? What outlets did you supply? There are significant differences between the way retailers buy compared with production companies and the general public. Did you deal in consumable products or capital equipment, or did you sell services? Let us consider the distinctions between the categories of products you might sell.

Capital equipment

This is an all-embracing term that might incorporate any size of machine, vehicles up to and including aeroplanes, and small add-ons to buildings, including air-conditioning and ventilation and the fabric of the building itself. The range is vast, but the nature of the sale has much in common in every case. The potential buyer is almost always a commercial enterprise, and most are buying capital goods either as a replacement or as part of an expansion programme. It is probable that several managers of different backgrounds will have some involvement in the decision, and that final approval will require director/board approval.

Smaller items such as computers or cars are relatively straightforward, but significant pieces of equipment will necessitate meeting a number of members of the management team, who are almost certain to be viewing competitive offers. It can take up to a year before negotiations are completed and the order is placed, and delivery of equipment can sometimes take a further year, so two years might elapse before any commission is earned.

Individuals who are successful dealing in larger, expensive equipment often have private means or substantial resources behind them, but there are many agents who have established strong businesses selling basic equipment like bottling or labelling apparatus, plant for the building industry, etc., where the price is in the range £10,000–£100,000. Commissions are typically 15 per cent, but they do vary according to what is involved and could be higher for agents who hold demonstration machines and deal in trade-ins and second-hand equipment.

A feature of this type of arrangement is that agents often sell foreign products: for example, they might have the UK agency for an Italian or American manufacturer. In such cases it is as well to recognise that if you are very successful, the principal may seek to replace you with an employee who costs less and who will take over the market you have created.

Against such a background you should try to establish a range of compatible equipment from different manufacturers. If, for instance, you have a bottling machine from Italy, it would be an advantage to represent a bottle-capping machinery manufacturer from Germany or elsewhere. You do not want to be totally dependent on one supplier.

It does help to have some basic industry knowledge and a reasonable technical background if you want to develop such a business. Ideally you would be able to use your contacts to ascertain what equipment is used and who supplies it. You could then approach manufacturers on the basis of your specialist knowledge and work out an arrangement.

You will probably need to be able to support yourself for up to a year before you have this type of agency business up and running, but a successful operation can be built up over time. These arrangements can, however, be a little volatile in the modern world, as companies sometimes defer capital spending in times of recession.

Selling services to industry

This covers a wide spectrum, from laundering and office cleaning to installation of vending machines and a range of maintenance and catering services, as well as insurance. Constantly repeating services need to be supplied locally, or through branch depots. Some of these may use commission agents to set up contracts, but margins are usually tight, so commissions rarely climb above 10 per cent and roll-over contracts may yield as little as 1 per cent. It is possible to achieve reasonable remuneration, but this area is more for the commission-type salesman than the former sales manager, as it offers little freedom of action and is a numbers game that must inevitably restrict creativity. Maintenance services and vending machines present some scope, but it is difficult to build your own customer base and ongoing relationships.

Insurance offers greater possibilities, although the law relating to commission on financial products is currently in a state of change, with proposals that agents should charge a fee for advice rather than earn a commission. Nevertheless, most companies need a package to cover potential calamities and to meet statutory obligations for third-party damage or vehicle insurance. Even quite small organisations find they soon have to shell out close to £10,000 per annum, and this figure increases as the company grows.

These products are also bought by the general public, so this is one of the few products that can be sold to virtually everybody. Many brokers therefore offer such products as a retail service and also have industrial clients. Specialising in either field can be lucrative, but industry knowledge across a wide range of products and suppliers is essential.

Selling repeating products

If you can find these opportunities, you can secure ongoing income. Most suppliers to industry tend to use their own sales forces to maintain links, and if they supply several products, particularly to manufacturers, multi-level contact is maintained. This is especially true of raw material supplies. Agencies do exist, but some provide a national sales force, usually when selling to retailers.

A particularly lucrative field is to marry design to agency arrangements and offer packages. Interior designers, for instance, provide furnishing schemes that consist of carpets, curtains, furnishings, paintings and ornaments that blend together as a total package. In many cases they buy the products and hire fitters to hang wallpaper and curtains and carry out internal alterations, and charge a total sum that includes design fees and commission.

Similar projects can be put together for overseas manufacturing businesses in Africa or the Middle East, where an entire production line is sourced from different European manufacturers and assembled on site. Hotel refurbishing, to include air conditioning and security features, is another field of package scheme activities.

Selling to the public

In practice, this is a question of marketing rather than pure selling. Knocking on doors without knowing whether the occupier is a likely buyer or not is time-consuming and unpredictable. It evokes images of the commercial travellers of the 1930s. In modern times this has been superseded by party-plan selling and network marketing. Nevertheless, people do succeed with these businesses.

The overriding problem in selling directly to the public is market identification. In practical terms the options are to set up a retail business or to operate a direct-mail business, with or without the internet. I have described how to break into these businesses earlier in the chapter.

CHAPTER SIX
Studying and Defining Your Market

In every business it pays to find out as much as possible about the market you are operating in and to be aware of who your competitors are and what they are doing. This is taken for granted in most larger businesses, particularly where they hold a recognisable market share. Many smaller companies pay less attention than they should. I strongly recommend that you do some research before committing funds.

Products for the general public

With many start-ups, the choice of product defines the market. Conversely, you might decide to become involved in a particular market and then select a product that you believe has a place in such a market. In the latter case it is reasonable to assume that you already know something about the market. Even so, further research is desirable.

The market for many products is difficult to quantify, and even more difficult if you are working within a limited geographical area. Nevertheless, there is a surprising amount of information available.

Defining the market for products

The majority of products come into a general category that is then broken down into segments. If we take the market for toys, for instance, we can quickly ascertain the total value of toys sold in the UK in each of the last few years and possibly discern trends. This, however, is further subdivided into segments such as:

- Pre-school toys

- Dolls

- Board games

- Video games

- Outdoor games

It should be obvious which segment your toy falls into, and with a little research you can establish which companies are the main suppliers. With British companies you can quickly gain access to financial reports. You should also study their websites and find out about their complete range. This exercise will give you an overview of where your product fits and who the main suppliers are in the market sector. You might even be able to ascertain what share of the market the major companies hold. This will help to clarify whether there is room in the market for your particular product.

Comparing product features and benefits

The internet nowadays makes it much easier to study competitive products in detail. Most websites enable you to call up full product specifications and draw attention to particular features and how they benefit the customer. You should try to identify all products that are similar to yours and list their various features, then compare this with a list of your own product's features.

Unless you have something unique, which is rare in business, you are likely to be in competition from the moment you start selling a product. You must compare the features objectively. If your competitors clearly have more and better features, you probably have the wrong product, unless you are able to price it significantly more cheaply and still show adequate margins.

Selling the differences

This is a point I cannot stress highly enough. In all markets you should try and differentiate yourself. As far as possible you are searching for the unique sales point (USP). This is the advantage you are going to stress in advertisements, literature and sales pitches. Without it, you are inviting price competition that will put you out of business sooner rather than later.

If you carry out this research diligently and analyse the comparisons dispassionately, and conclude that you have identified features that competitors do not have but that are of benefit to customers, you can reasonably assume that you do have a marketable product. You also need to be confident that an adequate market exists.

Distributing the product

A further aspect of your study of competitors is to establish how the product is sold.

- Do competitors accept orders over the internet?

- How is the product priced?

- Are discounts offered?

- Do they sell to the general public through mail order?

- Do they sell through wholesalers and/or retailers?

- Do they advertise on TV?

- Do they have in-store demonstrators?

- Do they use point-of-sale materials, e.g. display cards in retail outlets?

- What other products do they sell?

Establishing the price

The price must be competitive if you hope to continue selling the product; hence you have to think carefully about your competitors' prices. Might your additional benefits enable you to charge a higher price, or are you content to match prices and try to outsell the competition?

Where you are selling a licensed product or one being manufactured on your behalf, you need to develop a marketing plan. (I will discuss marketing fully in the next chapter, as it is a subject that needs dealing with at length. At this stage we are still assessing product viability.) You must set a budget for this on an annual basis and a further budget for any other operating costs.

Calculating break-even

Calculate the gross margin by deducting the cost of the product from the intended price and divide the total budget by the margin to determine how many units you need to sell to cover the budget. You then have to consider promotional activity – special offers to boost sales – and recalculate how many units you need to sell to cover this additional cost.

Profit objectives
You are, of course, in business to make a profit. At the very minimum you want to make a profit equal to your former salary plus additional funds to recoup your initial investment and cover the costs of any planned investment. If you truly cannot envisage achieving this, do not go ahead.

This section so far relates to a licensed product that you intend selling to the general public and/or through mail order. It also applies to a certain extent to specialist retailers, although retailing is part of the product supplier's means of distributing to the general public. It is reasonable to expect that they will have done similar market analysis. Specialist retailers should have continuous in-depth conversations with their suppliers about their market perceptions.

Analysing the industrial market
The general public is a self-evident description of a market. It can, of course, be analysed into segments by age, income, sex, and so on, and statistics relating to these categories, and many others, can be found. Precise definition, however, is difficult. It is relatively easy to find out how many pensioners there are in the UK, but virtually impossible to know where they all live. The same is not true of industry. Let us therefore begin by thinking about the various types of businesses under a variety of headings.

Public quoted companies

There are approximately 3,000 companies quoted on the London Stock Exchange. The hundred largest are usually referred to as the FTSE, and this group almost certainly excludes any business with less than £1.5 billion in annual sales and ranges to vast international businesses with in excess of £100 billion sales. In reality, most of these businesses are large groups of companies with several subsidiaries, some of which may themselves have sales of a few billion.

The next four hundred quoted companies are classified as large and almost certainly have sales in excess of half a billion per annum. As such, they too are adequately resourced and only likely to engage individual professionals with highly specialised abilities. All these companies are an unlikely market for the solo operator.

Small and medium-sized enterprises (SMEs)

This category includes the other 2,500 or so quoted businesses, almost all with sales of more than £100 million per annum. These companies are often structured as groups and may occasionally utilise interim managers or individuals on a project basis but more usually tend to employ established management consultant practices or teams of individuals.

Some smaller businesses are quoted on the Alternative Investment Market (AIM). These have usually raised expansion finance and see AIM as a stepping stone to a full quotation on the London Stock Exchange. Some of these businesses ultimately fail, and it is not unknown for major quoted companies to crash completely.

I do not know the actual figure, but it seems likely that public quoted companies account for in the order of 70 per cent of the UK economy, although there is an increasing amount of foreign ownership of British companies.

The private sector
The UK has in excess of four million businesses registered for VAT, ranging from individuals to substantial private companies.

Industry sectors
The national economy breaks down into major and minor industry sectors – food, construction, finance, transport, leisure, engineering, etc. Each has several sub-sectors. If we take food, we can immediately think of:

- Fresh food

- Frozen food

- Canned food

- Cereals

- Bread and flour confectionery

We can further subdivide the sub-sectors into:

- Fruit

- Vegetables

- Meat

- Fish

- Processed foods

There is published information on all these sectors and sub-sectors, so it is easy to choose the best areas for your products or services, and also to identify all the potential clients in each sector and break this down further into geographical regions.

> **T**his is the starting point for all redundant managers who choose to develop a business built on their own professional skills or providing products to operating companies.

Creating a database

The major advantage in selling to industry is that you are able to define your market quite closely. This also means that you can, in many cases, target your message at specific individuals. It follows that you should hold this information on a computerised database and evolve a system that will enable you to communicate with potential and existing customers and clients.

Information can be obtained from a variety of sources. A number of firms provide company details that include:

- Nature of the business
- Address
- Telephone numbers
- Email addresses
- Names of directors
- Website addresses
- Turnover

- Profits

- Number of employees

This information is available to rent, rather like list brokers, and can be analysed by:

- Industry sector

- Geography/postcode

- Turnover range

- Number of employees

It is possible to acquire a database appropriate to your needs and to build this progressively. You might decide, for example, to concentrate on all manufacturing companies with sales of at least £1 million, employing more than twenty personnel, based in Yorkshire. You could almost certainly acquire this information on disk within a matter of days.

I strongly urge anybody who is intent on supplying products or services to industrial customers to make this investment in an appropriate database and to keep it up to date. The way you use it will vary according to the nature of your business. This, too, is a subject that will be referred to constantly as we proceed.

Finding a market for professional services

Professional services by their nature are used by both the public and business communities. Few practitioners are adept at handling both, as the nature of the client relationship differs in each case. With the general public you are usually dealing with an individual client, whereas companies often have their own specialists and departmental managers who might be involved at various stages. It should probably be an early decision to choose which sector you wish to work in.

A local service

As stated earlier, professional services now encompass a wide range of activities. The best way to find a niche in which to specialise is to study the competition for the gaps in what is available. This is relatively straightforward, as most professional practitioners act within a small geographic area. Certainly the public are unlikely to travel fifty miles to see a dentist or lawyer. Most industrial clients would expect you to visit them, so you would not want to travel a long distance for a short meeting.

Studying the competition

The public has a general perception about what professionals do, and often rely on recommendations from friends or other specialists when in need of their services. Many people find it difficult to differentiate between one doctor and another. The same applies to solicitors, dentists, etc. This perception is difficult to overcome, but in reality, most professionals have something that sets them apart. If we take the case of solicitors, many of whom enjoy the variety of general practice, we find that their advertising focuses increasingly on specific subjects – family law, property conveyancing, litigation, crime, etc. This does not mean that they will not attempt to handle other matters; just that they have built their reputation in a particular field.

In determining how to present yourself in the market when setting up initially, it pays to look for a niche, or some add-on that draws attention to you. An architect might say:

'House extensions a speciality', or a dentist might focus on cosmetic surgery in any literature produced. You should therefore study competitors' websites to see what they are doing and where they are located. In many ways this is similar to studying competing products. You need to find that edge that draws people's attention.

The major point about differentiation is that it helps to justify prices. If everybody is perceived as being the same, then most people would choose the lowest price on offer.

Offering professional services to businesses

It is the growth of commerce that has brought about the newer professions. Accountancy emerged around 150 years ago, but is a mere youngster compared with doctors and lawyers. Management consulting started between the two world wars, primarily with studies aimed at efficiency improvements. It has grown substantially with services such as systems analysis and management recruitment. IT services, however, have only become recognised in the last twenty years.

This growth has also enabled lawyers to provide legal services to commerce and opened opportunities for architects and insurance brokers, many of whom are still generalists.

Defining the business market

As described above, the range of businesses is extensive, and buying practices vary according to the nature of each business and what it is procuring. Generally speaking, capital expenditure is decided at the top of a business, and the decision may require input from several managers and ultimately even group board approval. Stationery, on the other hand, might be ordered by a secretary.

There is massive diversity, and you need to try and determine a sector where your services could fill a gap. A lawyer might offer a debt-collecting service, but probably not to Shell or Glaxo. In all probability it would work best for a smaller local company where contact is easily maintained and the procedure could be standardised, streamlined and made cost-effective.

Many IT consultants still wait to be consulted. The more proactive decide what they do best and focus on their chosen niche. It might be building websites and helping clients get the best out of them; or advising what software systems to buy after analysing requirements and then helping to train staff in their use. Again, you are not going to sell these services to Ford Motors or General Foods.

Creating a database

As we saw above, a database is essential to agents dealing in specific products that are sold to businesses. It will be equally necessary to consultants offering management services. Those of you who intend operating professional practices should find this a helpful aid in promoting yourselves. To my mind it is one of the best tools available to smaller businesses and is in constant use by major marketing companies.

First, however, you must define your likely market. If, as seems most likely, you are setting up a local business, you should perhaps consider all businesses within a twenty -mile range of your premises and then introduce further qualifications. An architect will want to find customers who need sizeable premises, thereby ruling out skilled trades who do most of their work on their customers' premises. Alternatively he might start by ruling in manufacturing companies, warehouse and distribution businesses, private clinics and various stockists, for instance. This leaves the option open as to whether to enlarge his database later by extending the geographic range or focusing on particular types of business across a much larger region.

The desired upshot is that you have obtained good, usable information about, say, a thousand businesses, many of whom could become prospective clients.

> This is a target market, clearly identified, and capable of being fine-tuned progressively and easily expanded if desired.

Defining the market for management services

> This business is in its infancy but is capable of expanding rapidly as operating companies run on minimum staffing and resort to occasional hire. It is a major opportunity area for redundant managers.

Management consulting, as mentioned earlier, had its origins before the Second World War, when the USA and UK were big manufacturers with large assembly operations. As competition intensified, these companies sought improved efficiency and productivity. This in turn brought a demand for expert production engineers to observe, analyse and put forward reorganisation ideas. The concept boomed post-war, but as manufacturing moved to areas of cheaper labour, the consultants sought new fields and became involved in administration activities and systems development. This was aided by the introduction of accounting machines to process and analyse information more rapidly. Subsequently computers could handle information even faster and more efficiently.

Systems is probably the major part of management consultancy but the industry has moved into other fields too, such as business strategy, management recruitment and training. The client base is multinationals and large public companies where the fees are substantial but still modest compared with efficiency savings.

During the last twenty-five years or so, individuals have started successful businesses in activities such as recruitment and IT for smaller companies. Meanwhile, the major consulting firms have tailored some services for SMEs but are unlikely to be able to carry out projects economically in companies with a turnover much less than £10 million.

Trends in modern business

The search for improved efficiency is as old as the Industrial Revolution, but has intensified with globalisation and the faster-growing emerging economies. As a consequence, businesses in the UK and elsewhere have become much leaner. Two or three layers of management have been cut out of the tall pyramid organisations of thirty years ago. Structures are much flatter today, and more focused. This implies that they are not as capable of dealing with surges in activity and have less time for analysing what is going on in the business. There are many worthwhile projects in most companies that could provide short-term employment for solo consultants and bring benefits to clients.

This is a further opportunity for displaced managers.

The market

Small business is badly served in the UK. Most companies are started by specialists who have a particular knowledge or skill and decide to launch out on their own. Motives vary. In some cases people feel they have no option other than to go it alone. Others want to be their own boss, while some are driven by ambition or necessity.

The first problem is usually finance. People discover almost immediately that everything costs money, and they have to provide it. Banks will lend on security, but this often means pledging your home against a loan. The next discovery is that they also have to do everything else themselves, including finding customers, making or procuring the product, arranging delivery, invoicing the customer and handling the administration.

A high proportion of start-ups fail, sadly, mainly because they do not start out with a properly thought-through business plan and they have little idea about planning their finances. In short, they lack management skills. Many that do survive the early stages and establish some sort of market presence have just muddled through. Some are happy to do so, particularly if they are achieving a satisfactory income. These are unlikely to become an economic market for anyone other than the tax collector.

The second stage

Those who have pushed their turnover to say £750,000 are on the way. They are likely to be specialists, possibly good salesmen and probably achievers. Nevertheless, they have arrived at the point where ongoing growth will overwhelm them. They cannot afford to employ competent managers. Hiring an assistant often means you have two people doing the same job, and few know how to delegate properly. A surprising number of businesses grow annual sales from £1 million to £2 million over two to three years, but see no growth in profits and, quite often, a decline thereafter.

This is often an opportunity for a competent manager to become involved on a part-time basis and/or to carry out a project to help the business grow to the next stage.

Finding your niche

As a solo consultant (a term I will use from now on as it helps define this area of activity, which is not quite the same as management consultancy), you are unlikely to break into handling projects for public groups unless you have a high reputation or scarce specialist skills. This does not rule out working directly for group subsidiaries, but realistically, you should target yourself at the smaller business sector. I suggest you set a minimum level of sales of £750,000 p.a. to a ceiling of £10 million. (I have not quantified numbers recently, but my best guess is that the UK has approximately 500,000 companies that fit into this range.) A further quali-fication might be to add no fewer than five employees to rule out one-man trading companies.

As illustrated earlier in this chapter, this can be broken down into a large number of industry sectors that can be further divided into segments and even sub-segments. This facility enables you to determine quite closely those compan-ies where your skills might fit. If, for instance, you are a food technologist with several years' experience in the meat industry, you could, with a little effort and expense, iden-tify every meat processor and packer in the country. You will also want to narrow your market geographically to minimise travel, bearing in mind that you will need to meet every prospective client who expresses an interest in what you have to offer.

Building your database

You may find that suppliers of lists for your database have a minimum order of perhaps 1,000 names with details, but even a cost of a couple of thousand pounds is a small investment for information of this nature. Shop around and talk to companies who offer this service. In particular, ensure that the data is as up-to-date as possible. However many of these company names you acquire, I suggest you choose the 500 that seem most likely and focus on them initially. You might even grade your list into A, B and C categories.

You now have a closely identified target
market that should enable you to build a
successful business.

CHAPTER SEVEN

Defining and Implementing the Marketing Plan for Products

Many years ago, Unilever Group became the first UK listed company to spend £1 billion on advertising. When he announced this at the annual general meeting, the chairman said: 'We know half our money is wasted, but we don't know which half.' If Unilever, one of the most sophisticated businesses in the world, knows that it is wasting money, it is a warning to everybody else that this is an easy thing to do. Think very hard about what you are trying to achieve before you spend a penny. Be clear about your objectives.

Consider your options

One thing is certain: potential customers will not know about your product unless you find a way to tell them. We have already spent some time talking about identifying likely buyers, discussing this in relation to:

- Finding or creating a product you believe in

- Mail order

- Retailing

- Agency agreements

Each of these methods of bringing products to market varies significantly from the others, although the first two could be interchangeable, in that you could use a new product as a base for starting a mail-order business. There is some overlap, but each has a dominant method and uses other marketing tools as support. Let us therefore consider the choices available and how they relate to each of the above distribution methods.

Advertising

This is a general term that can be applied in a number of different ways and for a number of different reasons. Most of us are conscious of being blasted with mass-market advertising trying to entice us to buy a detergent for whiter clothes, escape to the sunshine for a family holiday, take out insurance cover for our cars, etc. The advertising is competing for our attention.

Mass marketing

Far more money is spent on this than on any other means of advertising. Products that most homes buy every week – food, toiletries, cleaning materials, beverages, etc. – fall into the category 'fast-moving consumer goods' (FMCG). This is an unlikely market for a recently redundant manager to operate in as a new start-up because of the enormous investment required to handle the volume. Most such businesses almost certainly have manufacturing plants.

The media used are TV commercials, hoardings, point-of-sale advertising in retail outlets, and occasionally radio. Most companies in these industries also have teams of sales representatives selling to retail outlets. The promoters are usually trying to establish or support a brand. The cost of doing so runs to millions.

Press advertising

This form of advertising encompasses much more than national and local newspapers. It also includes hundreds of magazines aimed at particular interest groups and trade journals for most industry sectors. The majority of these editions could not survive without paid-for advertising. These magazines are sold to specific readerships. Women's magazines dominate the market, but there are several other interest groups, including virtually every sport and hobby imaginable. Clearly, therefore, if you have narrowed your target market to a particular category, this type of advertising could pay off.

A word of caution is again necessary, because press advertising is expensive relative to audience in most cases, though much will depend on the nature of the product. You have to produce the advertisement yourself to a column inch size. This may necessitate photographs, copy and layout design, which alone could run to several hundred pounds before you have even paid for the space in the journal, usually a few hundred pounds more. It is also widely understood that an advert has to be repeated to have an effect. Readers have to see it a minimum of three times before they notice it, and possibly a couple of times more before reacting to it. This means its location could be critical. This too could affect price. Cover pages are usually charged at higher rates than inside.

The reality of press advertising is that you need to run the advertisement for at least six editions before you can truly judge the effect. You must therefore also consider how many people read the magazine and how to appeal to them.

Evaluating the response

The first comparison you should make when deciding where to place your advertisement is cost per reader, or per 1,000 readers. Clearly if one magazine charges £700 per two column inch and has 70,000 readers, the cost is £1 per 1,000. If the alternative costs £600 per two column inch, but only has 50,000 readers per month, the cost per 1,000 amounts to £1.20. If however you receive a 1 per cent response each time your product is advertised, the cost per order is £120. If the cheaper advertising only yields a 0.8 per cent response, the cost per order is £125.

This implies you must monitor the effect of every advertisement you place. You must also study trends: does the response rate improve the longer you continue advertising? Does it reach a peak and tail off? Does advertising help you make a profit?

Let us assume the product costs £30 to buy and £5 to deliver but you sell at £180 each. The situation would be:

	£	£
Sales price		180
Purchase price	30	
Delivery charge	5	
Advertising	125	
		160
Contribution to expenses and profit		20

You can see that variations in the cost of advertising could quickly eat away the margins, so close attention is essential.

Response rates can and do vary significantly. This may be due to a number of factors, including:

- Location, i.e. not easily seen

- Style and content – small changes can have a big impact

- Timing – holidays or a clash with a major event

- Price – not competitive, or perceived as cheap or expensive

The implications of these variables suggest that trying to do everything yourself is self-defeating, particularly when you lack experience. You should bring in professional designers and copywriters who have background knowledge in what you are trying to achieve. Having produced a professional advertisement, you must insist with the chosen magazine that it is appropriately displayed. If not, then threaten to terminate the contract.

If you have done your initial research thoroughly, you should be able to charge the right price. If not, hard reality will quickly teach you that there are no short cuts.

Making advertising pay

The type of advertising discussed above will help generate sales for both a single-product marketing and distribution company and a mail-order business. It also has a role to play for the retailer who recognises that he needs a back-up strategy to improve sales, and would have value to a sales agent who deals in specialist products that may appeal to a particular interest group, e.g. golfers or fishermen. However, as the sole means of promoting your business, it is unlikely to pay. You need to supplement it with other tactics.

One of the most important things to remember about this type of advertising is that having captured a customer, you must hang on to their details. Repeat business will help build your business profitably because it reduces the cost of obtaining sales. Ideally you will follow through by offering a further product, preferably a higher-priced item with a bigger margin. This is all part of the process for a mail-order business, whereby you insert a catalogue or leaflet with every delivery inviting the customer to buy something else. A mail order business is, of course, sending out direct mail to selected potential customers as a central part of its marketing strategy. PR is a natural addition to this form of promotion.

PR

PR can be a more cost-effective tool than advertising and often yields positive results. The purpose is to gain press coverage about your product. This can be done by writing articles and offering them to selected journals or magazines. Trade journals, in particular, frequently have only a skeleton journalist staff and are dependent on contributed material. This is often rewritten by the magazine, but most journals give credit to the product supplier and indicate where it can be obtained. If you enjoy writing and have some expertise, you can attempt this yourself, but it is time-consuming. You would also need to research particular magazines and study the nature and style of the articles they produce. This is usually a job for experts.

Many PR companies prefer to work on a retainer, whereby they commit a certain amount of time to your business. This helps them to understand more about the product and you.

The product must be interesting

It is almost self-evident that an article must catch a reader's attention and maintain their interest if it is to yield results.

This is easier with some products than others. Antique furniture, for instance, often has a history that can be woven into the article and possibly associated with an illustrious family. You could generate several interesting articles about this.

A swimming costume, however, presents more of a problem. A couple of paragraphs about its elastic waist would quickly bore readers. The focus would have to be more about holidays and looking good on the beach. Even then, it probably lacks a unique feature that a story could be built around. This is a further reason for studying the competition, as discussed earlier: to highlight differences that can be exploited. It is also a reason for using professional advisers.

Using your own background

Quite often a more interesting story can be built round you as promoter of the product, and how you scoured the world for the right item at a competitive price. If readers identify with you, you probably have them hooked.

Keeping your stories fresh

With this type of promotional activity, there is a risk of becoming stale. It is also a fact of life that magazines will not keep on accepting articles about subjects they have already described. This implies that you need to look for new angles and make sure that you are seen in a number of magazines focused on similar audiences. In this way you might be able to keep the story fresh over a few months and, once established, potential customers will know how to find you.

However, PR is rarely a major part of the marketing plan with most product-based businesses. Where it comes into its own is with service-based companies, as we will see in the next chapter.

Direct sales

In all probability in start-up companies you will be doing the selling yourself. Where you are marketing a single product to a sector of the public, direct selling is unlikely to apply, and it does not form part of a mail-order company by definition. As a retailer you will not have time to call on customers or hire a salesman to do so, unless you have something special to offer.

Direct selling is sometimes used with more expensive products like eighteenth-century marine paintings that could be sold to collectors, or period silver cutlery or artefacts. Even with these types of products you need to make a warm, expected approach rather than an unheralded call. This probably means an introductory letter or phone call.

Agency

This subject was covered in Chapter Five, where we discussed the types of agency that could be considered. The usual practice is to set up meetings through cold calling, or using a telesales agency. The meeting is a two-way communication whereby you try to ascertain the customer's needs and match your products against them.

The manner in which agency products are marketed to industrial users is similar to the way services are promoted. Indeed, agents are frequently used to sell services. This will be fully described in the next chapter.

Telesales

In many ways this is a substitute for direct selling. It is, of course, far less costly to make a telephone call than to have a salesman attend a meeting. Telesales can be used with both the general public and commercial businesses, and is employed mainly for durable products that customers buy once or replace every few years. Products that repeat regularly are best sold through retail.

This type of activity has grown dramatically in recent years, with much of it handled by Indian companies using computer links to reduce costs significantly. There is growing evidence that this tactic has peaked, particularly with the general public. Many people resent the intrusion and the persistence and aggression of callers. However, it continues to be used by many large companies, so it is probably still effective.

Lists and scripts

If the telesales process is to work effectively, it is vital that the agency is properly briefed and provided with a list of contacts who are likely to buy the product. If selling to a sector of the general public, you will need to acquire lists from brokers that attempt to identify potential customers. The agency then needs a script. This should be succinct and to the point. After a brief and polite introduction, the caller must quickly describe the product and the benefit it brings.

- Check that the respondent is the decision-maker

- State the benefits of the product

- Seek agreement that it is of interest

- Describe any special features

- Point out advantages against competition

- Quote price and ask for order

As far as possible, the agreement with the telesales agent should be structured on a price-per-order basis. The agency will want to cover its basic costs, but you need to add incentives to keep telesales personnel enthused. Costs can quickly mount, so if you are contemplating this as part of your marketing plan, you should carry out tests and measure results. You need to know:

- Number of calls made

- Number of decision-making contacts made

- Number of orders achieved

With this information you can calculate:

- How many contacts are needed per order

- How many names are needed per contact

- Cost per order

You are then left to decide if this is a profitable means of generating orders and how it compares with other selling methods.

Using the internet
In the modern age, a website is obligatory. Ideally it should be an active site, but circumstances vary according to what you are selling. If, as seems likely in the early stages, you have only one product, you have a number of jobs to carry out:

- Describe what the product does and what advantage that brings

- Differentiate it from the competition

- Make your business seem a credible supplier

If you have done all the preliminary analysis recommended in earlier chapters, you will have the answers to these questions and can be confident about your offer and why you are in business.

Thinking it through

The internet can be intimidating, particularly for the generation that has not grown up with these advances. You will probably need help. It is desirable to have somebody local who can unravel the intricacies and teach you the basics. Ideally you need somebody who understands the commercial objectives you want to achieve. Do not become carried away with all the potential of the web. It is a tool you can use to promote your product to a particular audience.

If you think in these terms, it will help you focus on the things that are essential to your plan.

Promoting through your website

Promoting your product to a recognised industrial market is relatively easy. It is much harder to attract a specific sector of the general public. The means at your disposal are search engines, which people use to find particular products and carry out comparisons. You can also use social media. This is more oblique, in that you are attempting to obtain recommendations through networks of like-minded people. They are likely to switch off if you harp on about your product, so messages need to be subtle.

Taking orders

This, perhaps, should be an early consideration. How will you take payment, process and deliver orders? A major part of the business will come in with credit card payments, which will necessitate opening a PayPal account. This is easy to do online, but the service costs money. You will also need to communicate the order to your fulfilment house or distribution centre. It is possible to set up automatic acknowledgements to orders, and this should be built into your system.

Capturing names

Be sure to retain the names and email addresses of all customers, including those who simply enquire or leave messages. This is your market identifying itself. The moment you introduce a second product, you should communicate the fact to the entire list. Depending also on the type of product you are selling, you should consider setting up a forum and send out regular messages. These should mention the product briefly but be more about showing you as someone who has the customers' interests at heart as a means of building trust.

Remember, it is always easier to sell to an existing customer than go out to find a new one.

The internet could merit a book on its own, and I will be writing more about the subject, and about database marketing, in the next chapter. I have also devoted a subsequent chapter to describing the types of businesses that can be developed solely on the internet. I do believe that it is a valuable tool that, if used wisely, can help you build your business. I also believe that it can become a serious distraction when people start to believe they can run a business with a computer and little else.

The internet is an enhanced means of communication, maintenance of records, analysis of results and systems coordination. Businesses are still run by people.

CHAPTER EIGHT

Marketing Services

In this chapter I want to make a distinction between established professional services and the more recent professions that have found a niche providing specific services to commercial clients.

Most people immediately recognise, in general terms, what solicitors, architects, doctors, accountants, stockbrokers and insurance intermediaries provide. Management consulting is also firmly established in the commercial sector, together with several of its specialist offshoots – recruitment, advertising, property management, etc. Many of the management professions, however, such as computer services, management accounting, graphic design and copywriting, are less well understood. Increasingly people with these backgrounds are finding interesting and remunerative project work with smaller companies. I also believe that a growing market is becoming available for other specialists, such as quality controllers, personnel managers and bank managers, who with a little initiative can create similar openings.

Marketing professional and business services
In the previous chapter, I discussed the tools that could be used to promote products. The same tools – advertising,

PR, telesales, etc. – can also be used in different ways to promote services. With products, there is an immense range and variety, so a certain amount of testing is necessary to determine what works best. With services, you can be more certain.

When marketing services to industrial or commercial clients, you have the enormous advantage of being able to identify your potential market quite closely, as described in Chapter Six. This enables you to empathise and to consider how you yourself would be influenced. Strangely, this is less true among the established professions because they also serve the general public, so let us consider them first.

The nature of professional practices

The professions now are dominated by a relatively few large organisations who focus almost exclusively on major corporations and government bodies. They tend to be centred in London, with satellite offices in major cities throughout the UK and, in many cases, internationally. Their fees are astronomical, judged by normal incomes, although lawyers up and down the country tend not to be shy.

Inevitably, some firms have joined forces over the years to form smaller, but significant, businesses. The majority of firms, however, tend to be local practices. Solicitors and doctors, in particular, still run general practices, backed by a referral system to barristers or consultants. Increasingly, though, many local practices have become specialists or have specialist partners. This is even more true of architects and surveyors.

The professionally qualified redundant manager who decides to revert to practice and has become somewhat specialised in his work would probably find this an advantage.

His background might be in employment law, contracts or possibly property, experience he could highlight when starting out afresh.

Starting a local practice

Being professionally qualified does not exempt anybody from carrying out the groundwork advocated in the first six chapters. Know yourself and your strengths and weaknesses, then study your sector and the competition. You are looking for a way into a tight-knit market that I will describe later in this chapter. Ideally you want to find a niche.

Architects and surveyors who have spent time employed by a commercial undertaking as opposed to a professional practice have probably worked for a multi-unit operation – retail outlets, pubs or distribution depots, etc. – and so have expertise in these areas. This is an obvious sector to target. Similarly a lawyer could offer a debt-collection service or an employment package of contracts and procedures. If you select this type of operation you are going to focus on an identifiable market and can therefore use the strategy I outline later in this chapter for services targeted at industry.

Generalists who intend to provide services to the general public should announce their arrival. Initially this should be local press coverage, where you write an article as a PR release, describing who you are and pointing to any gaps in the market that you will specifically cover. If there are several local papers, you could hold a small conference with drinks and canapés as a hook to attract busy editors and journalists. You need a big splash, so think it through carefully and consider backing it with a small advertising campaign for a few weeks. It would help if you could persuade an editor to accept a weekly article in his paper in which you write about modern design, or recent family case law, or what defects to look for when buying a house.

Considering the promotion mix

A **website** is obligatory today – most potential users of professional services will refer to this immediately. It must describe your background and experience and the services you offer. If you are able to include a few case histories, this would add to the interest. Doctors, solicitors and accountants must maintain clients' confidentiality and so cannot be specific about people. This limits what they can say about particular incidents, however interesting. Architects and surveyors may, with mutual agreement, identify clients and should be able to produce interesting case stories they can use.

Networking has been used by professional practitioners throughout the twentieth century and beyond and is a well-established means of generating business. I will describe it fully later in the chapter.

PR comes into its own with services, particularly in relation to industry. Capitalising on successes and building a story around them can be very effective. Readers like to identify with success. In many cases you can draft these stories yourself and send them to local editors, inviting them to use them in their papers. Writing local columns is even more effective.

Word of mouth is important and the means by which many established practices were originally built up. Most professions were not allowed to advertise until quite late in the twentieth century. A satisfied client will spread the word.

It is virtually impossible to measure the effectiveness of local advertising, so I would be inclined to exclude it.

Similarly direct mail and direct selling have no part to play, although when consulted by a client you are obviously in a sales situation. He needs reassurance and the confidence that you are able to provide the required service satisfactorily.

The background to the newer professions

Virtually all the businesses that fit into this category have emerged in the last 30–40 years. Some are even more recent. The occupations – graphic design, copywriting, management accounting, computer services, etc. – have existed for longer, but most of the people who did these jobs were full-time employees.

The trend towards leaner businesses is a modern practice that will continue for the foreseeable future. Few employers are able to ensure full-time work for everybody they employ. Employees also add to costs. They need working space, desks, telephones and computers; they incur a 13.8 per cent government levy for employers' National Insurance contributions and typically take five weeks' annual paid holiday, equal to another 10 per cent of their salary. In all probability the true cost of employment is likely to be at least 50 per cent more than the basic salary.

By avoiding these costs, employers can afford to hire specialists for projects or peak periods as they arise. They can also afford to pay more than the equivalent of a basic salary, because these self-employed practitioners bear their own overheads.

This is a golden opportunity for redundant managers. It offers:

- The chance to continue using the skills and experience gained

- Scope to operate from your own home at lower overhead cost

- A growth market

- Higher income opportunities

- Personal development

- Greater independence

Let us now consider how to break in to start and build a business.

Setting up a database

In earlier chapters we have dealt with defining your market, and pointed out that you can do so quite readily when you are providing services to operating companies. These are likely to be local businesses for most of you. I suggest you start with 1,000 names.

An internet search will quickly reveal companies who specialise in providing business information: I have used Dun & Bradstreet, who have an immense database of most UK businesses. Ideally, you want companies with a minimum turnover of £750,000. Anyone who has developed their business to this level is serious about it and plans to be around long-term. They also have reasonable cash flow and should be able to meet your fees. I think a ceiling of £5 million will suffice for most of you. Above this a company will attract the attention of established management consultants who can field teams of specialists, something you are unlikely to be able to compete with as a one-person business.

Your prospect details should include:

- Address, telephone numbers and email addresses

- Turnover for last three years

- Profits for last three years

- Number of employees

- Directors' names

- Associated companies, i.e. part of a group or not

This should be available on disk so that you can load it into your computer immediately.

Using the database

Try to resist the temptation to blast out emails to everybody. This is a target marketing exercise where your objective is to arrange meetings with the managing directors of companies on your list. It is important to concentrate on the person in charge, because appointment of senior personnel is nearly always a managing director decision. They may ask you to meet colleagues, but the final decision rests with the MD.

There are options regarding the initial approach. You could try a personal letter that briefly describes what you are offering. Follow up with a telephone call and insist on speaking to the boss. The advantage of writing first is that when the inevitable question comes demanding to know what the call is about, you can say in all honesty: 'It's about a personal letter I wrote last week.'

Once through, try to use a little smooth flattery, such as: 'I see the company has grown rapidly over the last three years. I assume this trend is continuing ...' You can then lead into talking about projects. You are not looking for a job.

Your proposition

As far as possible, you should try to package what you do as a series of projects:

- A systems review

- Installing a computerised planning and stock-control system

- Producing monthly management reports

- Compliance with Employment Acts

- Introducing quality-control standards

The point here is that you are implying a finite project that can be quantified. This provides comfort that you are not planning to be on the payroll in the long term. It allows you to follow through by discussing the benefits that would arise. If you can quantify both costs and benefits, with the latter being significantly more than the former, you have already hooked the client. It is hard for a business manager to turn down something that yields a profit.

> **Remember you must always stress benefits to clients. Unless some advantage is derived, there is no point in engaging you.**

You must imply that you have done some background research, but probe deeper to find out as much as possible over the telephone. Do not be afraid to ask about any problems the company faces. Remember, however, that your objective is a meeting, so do not say too much.

The early contacts are the hardest, so persevere. Once you have some success behind you, it becomes easier to back your story by quoting examples of how things worked out for other, unnamed, clients.

An alternative approach

Many people find cold calling quite difficult. It needs practice and confidence to pitch proposals about yourself to strangers. If this applies to you, then engage a telephone agency to set up meetings on your behalf (see p.82). If you go down this route, you should send a letter or leaflet to the prospective client, confirming the meeting and implying an agenda.

Using success stories

You should be able to build your business on success stories. By all means crow about them. If, for instance, you have completed a successful project for an engineering company, select all the engineering companies on your database and send the managing directors a brief email highlighting the salient points and describing the benefit derived by your client. When you have a few successes under your belt, you can write up the case histories as articles and ask local newspapers or trade journals to use them.

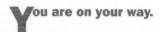

You are on your way.

Meeting clients

This is the most important aspect of your marketing plan; the moment of truth when you must secure the project.

Be smartly dressed, as though attending a job interview. Wherever possible, study the prospective client's website before you meet and learn as much as possible about the business. Have one or two questions ready; be relaxed and take control of the meeting. Once both parties are at ease, try to steer towards the substance of what you want to talk about. I find that asking questions is a good way to manage this, but we all have individual styles. Be yourself, and always be sincere

A possible conversation

Mike was waiting in the small reception area when the door opened and his host appeared in a white cotton jacket that bore the marks of working in the factory.

'Hello. I'm Henry Harding.' He extended his hand.

Mike gripped it firmly and smiled. 'Mike Smith.' He followed the slight, medium-sized man into a small, inexpensively furnished office with a cluttered teak desk.

'Sit yourself down.' Henry pointed to an upright wooden chair.

He obviously wasn't planning on a long meeting, Mike thought as he parked himself and took a few seconds to soak up the austere surroundings. 'You have the same name as the company, so I guess you're the founder?'

'That's right.'

'When did you start?'

'About fifteen years ago.'

Mike studied the man and figured he was under forty-five so had probably started before he was thirty. 'What did you do before?'

Henry grinned. 'I did an apprenticeship as an electrician. Went to night school twice a week and studied electronics. I worked for Ultra for a while before I figured I could do my own thing.'

'And you've built up to a turnover in excess of a million, I see.'

Henry raised an eyebrow. 'You've been checking up on us?'

'I get all the basic data to identify clients I am interested in and I had a look at your website.'

'It's a bit out of date and we don't know how to use it properly.'

'How many people do you employ now?'

'I have a dozen blokes in the factory and a couple of clerks. Rita is my PA. She does a bit of everything, and Molly, my wife, comes in two days a week to do the books and keep an eye on things.'

'She's a director too, I noticed.' Henry nodded. Mike continued, 'So you have your board meetings over dinner in the evenings?' He tried to keep it light-hearted but wondered to what extent Molly was a key part of the decision-making. 'What days does she work?' If this ran to a second meeting, he had better be sure to meet her.

'Tuesdays and Thursdays,' the founder replied. 'What is it you do?'

'I used to be HR manager with the XYZ Group until they threw me out, so I started my own business.'

'Doing what?'

Mike grinned and looked directly at Henry. 'Offering some of the experience I have gained in a large business to companies like yours.'

'Not sure I need it.'

'Well, for instance, have you got contracts of employment with everybody working here?'

'I agreed their wages with them all when I took them on.'

'And do you have standard terms and conditions?'

'They all work the same hours.'

'Have you had to fire anybody or go to short-time working? How about sickness?'

'I don't know about short-time working. We've been pretty busy lately. I did fire a couple of blokes last year. They'd been in the pub at lunchtime and were clowning around in the works with a forklift truck. A bit dangerous, I thought, so I told them to hop it.'

'Did either of them threaten you with a tribunal?'

Henry looked bemused. 'Threaten me with what?'

'It sounds as though you fired them without warning and you don't seem to have a disciplinary procedure.'

'So what?'

'They could go to court and sue for wrongful dismissal.'

'You've got to be joking.'

'Hardly. They could get several thousand pounds each.'

This is somewhat abridged, of course, and indicative only of how you could drive a conversation, but the essentials are there.

Impressions matter. Log them in your mind. Study the environment; it tells you a lot about your prospective client. The possibility that the founder's wife might have a strong influence on decision-making is also important. It could be a negative factor.

Your opening remarks are significant. Mike induced Henry to talk about himself and his business. This put him at ease, provided useful information and allowed Mike to ask more questions and guide the company's founder into talking about problems to which he has a solution. A short anecdote about another business that lost over £20,000 plus costs would probably be a clincher.

This type of conversation comes naturally to people who have been involved in sales. I frequently find people with a technical background to be a little disdainful about salesmen. Others are often shy and wait for the other party to speak first. The reality is that it is all about communication, and you must get your message through. You will be the one carrying out the project, so you must give the client confidence that you know what you are doing and that you will not upset everybody else.

> **It helps if you like people, because business is done by people. This is the moment when you win or lose. Try to be a winner.**

Keeping and using statistics

The best businesses have the best management. The best managers have the best information available. You are going to need information about your business too, if you are going to be effective.

If you are personally making calls, keep a record of whom you were able to speak to and whom you could not get through to. If you are a competent user of computers, you can build this into your system. If not, print out a list of names and note the details of each conversation. Mark those people you were unable to speak to. Note also the date and time you tried to call.

Let us assume you had a list of 50 names.

- You spoke to 15 people only

- 10 of them said they had no interest

- 2 said maybe at some future date

- 3 agreed to a meeting

Write immediately to the three people who agreed to meet, thanking them and confirming that you are looking forward to meeting them on the agreed date. Also write to the two who said maybe, confirming that you will call them again. Spend some time thinking about the people who said no.

- Why did they say no?

- Could you have put up a counter-argument?

- Did you find out enough about them?

- Could you improve your technique?

Do the same thing next time you spend a morning trying to make contact. After four or five contact periods, study the results to determine a pattern.

- How many calls do you have to make before you speak to a decision-maker?

- How many people do you talk to in order to set up a meeting?

- Is your technique improving?

- Are any trends developing?

Make a separate list of all the people you were unable to contact at the first attempt. Try contacting them again at different times of the day. If you cannot connect after three attempts, do not waste any more time on them.

This is your main marketing spend. Try to be as efficient as possible. As your business becomes more successful, you will be pressed for time but will probably always need to keep meeting new clients. You need to arrive at a point where you set aside an hour, make ten calls and achieve three meetings. When you can do that, the business will be humming.

Networking

This is a word that can be misunderstood. It is sometimes said of stockbrokers that they do more business on the golf course than they ever do in the office. You are unlikely to be in this position for many years to come. It is as well to remember, however, that everybody you meet might be a client or able to help you in some way.

Traditionally lawyers and accountants were never allowed to advertise for business. They had to rely on word of mouth, or on acquiring a reputation by subtle use of PR techniques – speaking on public occasions, writing letters to the press and meeting people in the community.

Using the local network

In virtually every town there are places or associations where professionals meet. Round Table has always been strongly supported by local estate agents, insurance brokers, solicitors, architects, surveyors and accountants. They run social functions and support charities. They all know one another quite well and make recommendations when in a position to do so. Typically somebody moves into the area and buys a house through a local estate agent. When the deal is confirmed, the buyer is quite likely to ask if the agent knows a good solicitor, who in turn recommends a surveyor, who suggests you use another friend of his to arrange insurance. It is a powerful network that captures a large share of new business purely by word of mouth.

There is absolutely no reason why the new professionals who offer services to industry – IT specialists, personnel managers, quality controllers, etc. – should not become part of this network. Indeed, it will pay them to do so and also extend their social lives.

Using satisfied clients

A job well done speaks for itself, but there is no reason why you should not lend a helping hand. Ask your client if he would mind recommending you to friends, or, alternatively, if you could refer prospective clients to him so that he can tell them what you did for him. As far as possible you should make friends with clients. They may want you to do other work for them at a future date. People find it easier to do business with people they like.

Building a professional network

This is an extension of the social network, whereby a management accountant knows a computer specialist he is able to recommend, or a designer knows a copywriter and they make a joint approach to revise a client's product literature. In the medium term, such arrangements will help you approach larger clients at higher fees, pulling a team together to carry out a bigger project. This, too, can have a social dimension. Over a period of time you will meet people at golf, tennis, cricket and bridge clubs, in amateur dramatic societies or at church socials. Do not be afraid to talk to them about what you do, and always think in terms of the benefits this will bring.

> **A**s a former redundant manager who elects to become a professional service provider or solo consultant, you are the product. As such, you are at the heart of promoting yourself to future clients and making a new life for yourself. Tackle it with enthusiasm and positivity.

CHAPTER NINE
Finding the Money

Your present situation

Most larger and more reputable corporations provide some cushioning by way of compensation to help lessen the shock of redundancy, particularly when downsizing to effect organisational changes that should show longer-term benefits. Redundant managers leaving these types of businesses will usually escape with close to a year's pay, the first £30,000 of which will be tax-free.

This isn't true of everybody, of course. At the bottom end of the scale, if the company has gone bankrupt or been forced into administration, you may receive nothing at all and therefore may be forced to take any moderately acceptable offer of employment in order to cover living costs. The average person leaving under redundancy terms should expect around six months' pay, including contractual notice and compensation. For most middle managers this sum would be tax-free, so probably equal to nine months' net salary.

This is, in most cases, a reasonable amount of time in which to find a new job. If, however, your thinking is moving towards self-employment, you need to decide quickly, because you are almost certain to need some capital. The amount will vary according to whether you wish to start a product- or service-based business.

Service or advisory-type businesses

Most single-person service businesses, based on your skills and experience, can be set up for well under £10,000 initially, but income will build progressively and it is likely to be a full year before you are spending most days of the week in a fee-earning role. Some occupations demand additional skills. This might oblige you to form a partnership or networking arrangement whereby you subcontract part of a project on an as-needed basis.

Budgeting your money

When you are faced with redundancy, the uncertainties of your situation mean that you must cut your living costs to eke out your resources for as long as possible. You should, therefore, start by analysing how you spend your money each month and decide what expenses could be eliminated. Thereafter you should plan what you need to spend month by month over the next year.

Try to assess what you need to spend to start your business – computers, printers, filing cabinets, market information, sales literature, etc. Add these costs to your budget and calculate how long you can last until you run out of money. This puts an immediate pressure upon you: 'I must produce income by ...'

The first and paramount objective is to generate income before you run out of money.

Product-based businesses

With product-based businesses, you are likely to need to buy stock. Simple ratios will guide you as to the likely investment: e.g. what margin will you achieve and how many times will you rotate stocks annually? If we apply this to a simple retail business, where you mark up purchases by 50 per cent and turn stock round every two months on average, then a £30,000 investment in stock will generate £180,000 in annual sales, of which one third, or £60,000, will be gross profit. This margin will have to cover rent, rates, light and heat as well as provide an income. With this type of business you would also incur further upfront investment in shopfitting, shelving, lighting and so forth.

Retail is not the only way to sell products, of course. As described in earlier chapters, you could be an agent for somebody else's products, or sell through mail order, using a fulfilment house to stock and deliver products at a much lower investment cost.

Acquiring a business

There are further options with both services and products. You might elect to buy a ready-made business that is outside of your professional experience, but about which you have some knowledge and understanding: a hobby shop, for instance, or a country pub, or a retail service business like a dry cleaner's or a motor repair centre.

There are certain attractions about buying a ready-made business, provided the price is right. Not only is the risk much lower than a start-up, but you gain an immediate income. On the down side, most vendors and their agents think a business is worth more than its true commercial value. You are likely to need professional advice from lawyers and accountants in evaluating the business and drawing up contracts (this subject was discussed fully in Chapter Four).

Business structuring

Initially you should act as a sole trader, or, if your spouse or partner wishes to participate, you could form a partnership. Partnerships do not have to be an equal share; they can be anything you want them to be, but this needs to be put in writing. You could, for instance, agree that one party has 5 per cent commission on sales, but only 20 per cent share of profits, or split profits 60:40. One partner may put up cash and could be paid interest on the investment before profits are divided in whatever proportion you agree on.

Whether operating as a sole trader or in partnership, you become personally liable to repay any borrowings, so all your assets are at risk. This will apply in partnerships even if the agreement states that one party only is responsible for repaying any loans. Banks or creditors are free to seek repayment from either party if the business assets no longer exist. It will be for the partners to remedy the situation later. This is a serious potential down side to partnership arrangements: if one partner goes bankrupt, the other is responsible for any outstanding liabilities of the partnership.

Limited companies

The liabilities of limited companies are restricted to the capital and reserves. This means that if you start a business with £1,000 that you convert into 1,000 shares of £1 each, that is the only money the company has. If the business runs up £3,000 of debt that it cannot repay, the creditors can only act against the company and cannot sue the directors or owners personally. In practice, banks, and sometimes other creditors, get round this by lending on other security that you provide, or seek a personal guarantee from the directors and/or owners that they will become personally liable if the company defaults. Notwithstanding this arrangement with banks, you are usually protected from action by other creditors if the business fails.

There are tax advantages in operating through companies and partnerships that I will describe later.

Raising bank finance

When considering buying a business, it is likely that you will need to borrow money to conclude the deal. Borrowings are normal in business, but your attitude towards risk – and indeed your spouse or partner's attitude towards risk – should be part of the self-awareness analysis you perform before making any decision, particularly where the sums involved are significant. For most people, the only asset they can pledge is the family home, and if you do put this up as security, you must be under no illusions. You could lose it.

It may be that you are able to borrow money within the family, but for most people the bank is the first port of call. We are in difficult times at present, but normal business banking policy is to lend money on security. In many cases they will view the business you are buying as part of that security.

Let us assume that the bank accepts the business is worth £75,000 and expects you to put up hard cash of £25,000, depending on the view taken of your business plan, and your own income requirements. They would want to be assured that you have sufficient income to meet interest on the loan and repay borrowings over a five- to seven-year period. The presentation of a business plan is of critical importance to the bank and also a good discipline to help you think through all the considerations of how you will manage and develop the business as well as your lifestyle choices. Do you want to send the kids to university? Do you need to run two cars?

A further possibility for raising capital is to increase your mortgage. Most home owners have received a windfall over the last ten to fifteen years due to house price inflation. Remortgaging is likely to be a cheaper option than borrowing from a bank, and avoids pledging the business assets. Building societies do not like lending in order to finance businesses; technically they provide loans to acquire domestic properties, but since most building societies have been taken over by banks, the lines are becoming blurred.

Convincing the bank manager

As with most things in life, you have to try and understand the other person's point of view. Banks need to lend money but do not want to lose it. It follows that they need to be reassured that you are an honest person who runs a successful business – or, if not yet started, that you are capable of doing so. They will usually ask you to provide a business plan or finance proposal, setting out your expectations and requirements, defining how the money will be used and how funds will flow through your business, and, of course, how it will be repaid.

Most bank managers will want to know something about you and what assets you have. Take your CV along with you, and a statement of assets and liabilities. This should show that you are solvent and have net assets that you are willing to pledge in support of the business, if necessary.

This does not in any way imply that you have to keep

going until all your assets have disappeared. It does, however, offer some reassurance to the bank that they can look to you to repay their loan if the business fails. Bankers are also more likely to support somebody who displays confidence and is willing to take a risk.

The finance proposal

Unless you have experience of preparing these plans, you will need to sit down with your accountant and write it together. Your accountant cannot be expected to know your trade or much about the markets you operate in, so you will have to prepare these sections yourself. The accountant's input will be more about cash-flow statements and calculating how much you need and how quickly you are able to make repayment.

The plan should start with a summary giving two sentences on the background and stating how much money is needed, and what for, followed by a short paragraph on the market and how it will be exploited due to particular advantages. The next paragraph should highlight, in tabular form, sales less expenses to show net profits for each of the three years ahead. If you have historical figures, show the two most recent years. In the final paragraph you should state the peak funding requirement and the length of time needed to repay, and ask for the money.

There should then be around one page of typed A4 paper on each of the following:

Background. Who are you? What experience do you have? Why are you going into business? How do you see the opportunities ahead of you?

The market and competition. Who are you intending to serve or supply? What are the going rates and/or prices and margins? Who are the established competitors and how do they operate? Have you found a niche you can specialise in supplying? How will the market develop over the next few years?

The marketing plan. How will you promote the business? What advantages do you have over existing competition? How will you exploit them? What contacts do you have? How will you price the product/service? What resources do you need to carry out the plan?

Trading projections. Sales forecasts for three years, less expenses to show net margins and net profits.

Capital expenditure requirements. How much are you paying for the business? What else are you planning to buy, e.g. computers, printers, database, furniture and fitments, car, etc.? What do they cost? How much are you contributing to the whole? What additional security is available?

Cash-flow projections. These should set out the timing of expenditure month by month and the progression of monthly sales, reflecting the difference between income and expenditure. Ideally they should show peak borrowings during the first six months that are gradually reduced as income grows until repayment is made.

The whole needs only to run to five or six pages, plus three pages of cash-flow projections, and should be neatly typed and presented in a folder, with an extra copy for the bank manager in case he has to refer it. Generally I prefer to bring these documents with me rather than send them through the post. Business is actually done between people and it is as well to present yourself and talk about your business with a measure of enthusiasm, guiding the manager through the sections and answering his questions. If you are dealing with the bank at a sufficiently senior level, you will probably receive an immediate decision; otherwise, it may take a few days.

Other forms of finance

The bank is your first option and, generally speaking, the least expensive, because they take security and usually expect to receive regular reports. They are also in a position to monitor your income and expenditure and therefore react quickly if they sense something is wrong.

Other lenders are frequently used to provide specific types of finance – asset purchase, export trading and debt finance. Let us consider briefly how these options may be used.

Factoring

Under factoring arrangements, the debtors of the business are assigned to the finance provider as soon as sales are invoiced. The factor provides, typically, 70 per cent of your total debts and takes over the management of your sales ledger. This means they also collect cash from your customer that is accounted for, and the total facility is adjusted on a daily basis. Interest is computed daily and a management charge is applied for the service. Any debts not collected within a reasonable period of time are referred back to you to chase and deducted from the loan facility. The effect of this is that the factor provides you immediately with 70 per cent of the cash owing to you, rather than you having to wait for your customers to pay you later.

It is implicit in the agreement that your debtors are not already pledged as security. Banks usually take what is known as a 'fixed and floating charge' over the assets of the business. This automatically incorporates a charge over your debtors. If you have already entered into such an arrangement, you cannot pledge the debtors a second time. You might be able to persuade your bank to release the floating charge over debtors, or in some circumstances replace your overdraft with a factoring service.

Overall this arrangement is more expensive than a bank overdraft because of the management charges. It is also made obvious to your customers that you are using this type of finance. This begs the question as to *why* you might use it. The usual answer is that it provides finance for profitable expansion. Where sales are growing quickly, a fixed overdraft limits your ability to expand. Factoring is a more flexible source of funds. As your debtors grow, your available facility grows, but you only receive 70 per cent of this expansion in debtors. You therefore need high margins to maintain this growth.

This service is not available when dealing with the general public, but could be ideal for a rapidly expanding trading company.

Import and export finance

This again is a specific type of finance, almost certainly not available to new start-ups, which can be used as a form of bridging.

Most importers have a problem in that overseas suppliers usually demand a letter of credit (LOC) with the order for goods. The LOC is raised on your bank and guarantees payment to the supplier once goods are satisfactorily received. The bank, of course, requires upfront payment before issuing a guarantee, or alternatively deducts the amount committed from your overdraft facility. This frequently means that funds are tied up for more than three months awaiting delivery of goods before you can sell them.

This gap has been seen and understood by acceptance houses, who will provide trade finance on security of the goods in transit until sold. This is almost tantamount to financing the LOCs and is, of course, a revolving facility, as you might have a number of LOCs at any one time. There is an implicit risk in this situation, so the facility is only available to substantial businesses with an established trading record. Such companies can sometimes use 'bills of exchange' rather than LOCs and possibly negotiate a line of bills with international banks.

Asset finance

Hire purchase and similar arrangements have been around since the end of the Second World War. Such schemes are widely available and are arranged in such a manner that they are additional to bank borrowings, as the security is taken by the prime lender before they pass into your ownership.

In simple terms, you merely pay a deposit on purchase and agree to pay the balance by instalments over a period of time. Full ownership is assigned to you when the final balance is paid. Interest is built into the instalments and the overall effect is to spread the cost of the asset over a number of years. Technically this is capital expenditure, so instalments cannot be offset against income for tax purposes. The interest is allowable, however, and depreciation allowances can be claimed.

It is a convenient way of acquiring assets provided you have sufficient income to cover instalments.

Venture capital

Both government and the finance industry have long understood that small businesses have serious difficulty in raising adequate finance. Several initiatives have been introduced over the years, most of which have proved expensive. No satisfactory solution has emerged, despite a number of study groups staffed by eminent figures from business, finance and government.

In simple terms, the problem is in three parts:

- Owner managers are obliged to surrender a measure of autonomy

- Investors want an exit route, usually within five years

- Investment requirements are relatively small sums in financial terms and difficult to monitor efficiently

Before considering the venture capital route, you need to look hard at the implications of these three constraints:

- Are you willing to take a financial partner into your business?

- Do you acknowledge that such persons will want a say on policies?

- Do you recognise that their exit will almost certainly lead to the sale of your business?

It is implicit in the questions that the purpose of raising this type of finance is to make it possible to build a much larger business than could be achieved without access to the money. You would have a smaller share of a much larger enterprise, but would expect to benefit significantly in financial terms.

The professional investment industry

Massive sums of money move through the hands of pension funds and insurance companies every day. The fund managers have to find an immediate home for this. They cannot afford to leave this money lying around not earning. Equally they cannot afford to make rash investments.

In practice they have created a number of subordinate funds that subscribers choose to put money into, such as government bonds, UK equities, emerging markets, North America, etc. Investment managers are supported by teams of analysts who become specialists in these markets and identify specific opportunities within their chosen fields. In effect, the choices are made before the money arrives. The equity investment targets are large companies, usually FTSE 100 companies in the UK, or leading businesses where other active markets exist and 20–30 million shares change hands every day. This liquidity, as it is known, is of vital importance, as circumstances can change within short periods of time and managers may need to dump holdings or buy in more stocks. They are busy people, watching their screens intently and making multimillion-pound decisions all day long.

Against this background, it can be seen that a fund manager does not have the time or the facility to consider small investments in private companies where there is no market for the shares.

The venture capital industry

This industry grew out of the recognition that small companies need finance to grow larger, and that some jewels exist. Inevitably, it, too, has split into specialist firms that only operate in sectors they have experience of, or situations where they have knowledge.

Even in this industry there are several companies that are looking for more secure, solid investments, such as management buyouts where groups choose to divest themselves of businesses that do not quite fit their overall strategy.

The firms that deal in smaller investments, possibly under £1 million to about £5 million, tend to be made up of practical, experienced managers who have a stake in the firm and have established a small team. They secure an allocation of funds from the major investment managers, who treat it as a single venture and do not worry about the detail. The reality of these businesses, however, is that they make only two to five investments annually. They are not risk averse – many have experienced total write-offs in the past – but they are looking for high growth prospects and it is rare for them to invest in start-ups.

The general requirements are to find businesses that show steady growth and have a track record of increasing profits. Typically it takes nine months to approve an investment. The investment manager charges for his time in analysing the market and making and evaluating plans, and expects to appoint a non-executive director to the board of the investee company.

I estimate that the venture capital industry provides development capital to fewer than 1,000 UK companies every year.

Raising smaller sums

In a number of towns around the country, networks of businessmen with money have been created to help provide small amounts of capital for businesses that could grow. Some are just local funds that provide modest sums of say £30–100,000, purely as investments; others ask individuals to act as 'angels', whereby they take a stake in the business and play a part-time management role. Such investors usually have relevant industry experience.

Corporate partnering

This is less common but could apply to those of you who have something new to offer, particularly in terms of products. Agreements can sometimes be negotiated with large corporations to provide funds to enable you to develop your business and establish the product. Such companies would usually seek to buy you out, once successful.

Keep trying

I have covered this subject at some length because most small businesses find it difficult to raise adequate finance and blame the banks or the system. I actually believe that finance is available for any properly managed business that has clear objectives and comprehensive plans of how to achieve them. The sums should add up; the presentation should be crisp. If you are turned down, there is usually a reason. Ask why and think about the answer. If necessary, change your plans slightly to accommodate the negatives and take them to a different bank or investor.

> **I**nvestors will probably require some sacrifice
> **f**rom you. They have reasons for asking.
> Do not blame them if you are unwilling
> to take some risk too.

CHAPTER TEN
Record Keeping and Administration

Essential accounting records

Modern accounting should not be seen as a mystery. Most small businesses can maintain adequate records on spreadsheets in a manner that is both simple and informative. In all circumstances you should, however, open a separate bank account for the business.

The following general guidelines will apply to all service-based businesses, though there is inevitably a great deal of complexity in taxation law.

Sales records

Invoices should be issued for items supplied or services rendered, with copies retained. You should list these showing the date raised, with an adjacent column where you enter cash received and a further date alongside. In this way you can see at a glance who owes you money and who has paid.

Your invoice should state boldly when you expect to be paid: e.g. 'Cash on delivery' or 'Payment due in 15 days'. There should be no doubt about payment terms and you should make a practice of chasing people who have not paid what is due.

If so desired, your sales record could have additional columns for any product or service analysis. This is helpful to you and shows what is selling.

Expenditure

A spreadsheet should be maintained with payments registered under headings such as 'telephone', 'office supplies', 'travel expenses', etc. You might also need a column for VAT, if you are registered and able to offset VAT paid against VAT added to fees. The figures should be totalled monthly so that you can see clearly what you have spent in full and in detail.

The nature of expenses

The Inland Revenue will allow the expenses involved in running the business to be set off against income as long as they are 'wholly and exclusively incurred'. In practice they will allow some apportionment between private and business expenditure, though increasingly they demand receipts or evidence of such expenses. It is important, therefore, when expenditure is incurred on behalf of the business, that contracts and invoices are made out in the trading name. This is particularly true of mobile phones, which *must* be in the business name. Other expenses are discussed below.

Rent of rooms/offices

If you own your own house, part of which is used for business purposes, there is little point in charging the business a rent, as the IR will deem such rent as income in your hands and add it to other income to levy tax on you. If, however, you are renting office space directly from a third party, the full rental and rates should be charged to the business together with operating costs, heat and light, etc. Again the property lease should be to the company, if incorporated, not you as an individual. Where you rent your house and use a room for business purposes you may charge part of the rental to the business. The Revenue will, in all circumstances, allow a nominal charge for business use.

Motor cars
Under current tax law, it is no longer worthwhile buying a company car that is mainly used as a private vehicle. Instead business mileage can be charged at 45 pence per mile for the first 10,000 miles and at 25 pence per mile thereafter. This necessitates keeping records of business trips and invoicing the business monthly. The business should then reimburse you. (This clearly implies that you should open a separate bank account for your business.)

Travel and subsistence
Out-of-pocket expenses incurred on business should again be reimbursed, but receipts should be obtained. This can include hotels, train fares, lunches and beverages, etc. Again these should be scheduled, with receipts attached, and borne by the business.

Other expenses
Newspapers, technical journals, reference books, postage, telephone calls, parking and beverages can all be charged as business expenses. Receipts should be attached where available. It should be noted, however, that entertaining is specifically not allowed as a deduction.

Employment of staff

Ideally any employees should be hired and paid by the business and you should deduct and account for PAYE and National Insurance and pay employer's National Insurance also. Once you have three or four employees, it may be worth acquiring a simple computerised system that will keep individual records of employees to be used for annual returns. Most accountants will handle this for you.

There is merit in employing spouses at up to £645 per month currently, if they do not have other employment and provided they carry out some small functions like keeping records, answering the telephone, filing, etc. If more seriously involved with the business, they could be paid more. This has the effect of diverting higher-taxed income from you to your spouse or partner.

VAT

You must register for VAT within thirty days of your sales or fees reaching £77,000 within any twelve-month period. You have the option to register at a lower figure if you wish to do so.

Bank reconciliation

The spreadsheets showing bank receipts and bank payments must record everything that passes through your bank account. You should check them monthly to be sure you have picked up any standing orders or direct debits and bank charges. The total of your income less expenses should agree with the balance shown on your account. This practice helps to verify the accuracy of your records.

Where you are dealing with cash, as in a retail business, you need to log cash received and bankings and keep a cash payments spreadsheet in addition to the bank payments one.

Budgeting

It is sensible to break your annual plan down into a monthly budget whereby you set out what you expect to earn in fees or charge as sales. You should prepare a similar schedule of anticipated expenses. You can quickly compare your actual expenditure against this every month to ensure that you have made reasonably close estimates and that your expenditure is under control and in line with your expectations. If not, you need to ask yourself why and, if necessary, recast your budget to assess the overall effect on your plans.

The point of this exercise is so that you can take action before you run out of money.

Communications with customers

Service businesses should keep client files. Over a period of time you will find you need a record of your dealings with clients. Increasingly these can be computerised files. Confirm all meetings in writing. Maintain a weekly log of what you have been doing for clients. Where projects have been agreed, set out in writing:

- What you have undertaken to do

- The support you will need from the client

- The records that need to be available to you

- The start date and likely timescale

- The fees agreed and payment schedules

Keep copies of any reports produced.

In retail and mail order or internet businesses, you are dealing with the general public so do not need individual records, but you should ensure slick service and keep your image polished.

Monitoring activities within the business

Statistics are important sources of information in any modern business, where the need to be efficient is increasingly obvious. I have already discussed measuring the effectiveness of database marketing, which shows you how much it costs to obtain a single client. This is useful information and something you should strive to improve. In a service-based business, you need to maximise the chargeable time spent working for clients.

With products, we have also talked about measuring the effectiveness of each and every advert. It clearly pays to know the most efficient way to obtain results. Trends here are important too, in that constant advertising can quickly achieve saturation and become less effective.

For the first 6–12 months of your business career, you should keep daily time sheets to record how you are spending your time, particularly in a service business. As you become more successful, the pressure will build and you will need to deal with more tasks, more efficiently. You need to organise your activities to create as much chargeable time as possible.

Business planning

If, when starting out, you needed to raise money, you will have had to formulate a business plan in support of your request. In any case, it is good practice, and any plans you produce should be constantly reviewed and updated.

Many years ago, the government introduced a loan guarantee scheme, whereby they would guarantee 80 per cent of a loan to a small company if a bank agreed they would normally lend but the client had insufficient security. This concept ultimately cost taxpayers a substantial amount of money. The results were analysed and the main findings were that small businesses that failed generally speaking had inadequate plans and poor accounting records.

This analysis brings us almost full circle. You must:

- Set practical objectives

- Make realistic plans to achieve them

- Monitor and review progress

- Revise plans or take new initiatives to reach your goals

Complying with government requirements

The government has imposed quite onerous obligations on commercial undertakings, and despite the protests it shows little sign of letting up. The construction industry, in particular, has been obliged to set up special departments in order to comply with health and safety regulations. I doubt very much whether most small builders know all the various building regulations that apply throughout the land. A significant proportion certainly don't understand some of them. And then there are all the obscurities of gaining planning permission in the first place ...

Health and safety

Health and safety regulations now impinge on every business. The Workplace (Health, Safety and Welfare) Regulations of 1992 is probably one of the most expensive acts that ever found its way on to the statute book and has had many adverse effects. Despite this, it has never been amended, and every town council in the UK now employs a health and safety officer. For the most part you can ignore the regulations while you remain a sole practitioner, but as soon as you employ people, you will be obliged to comply. I suggest that when you do, you invite the local officer round to advise you about your obligations.

Business registration

You must register with HM Revenue & Customs (HMRC) within three months of starting out in business. Go to the HMRC website and follow instructions. This will trigger a direct debit from your account for National Insurance contributions at the rate of £2.70 per week in 2013–14, paid monthly.

You do not need to register for VAT until you achieve sales or fee income in excess of £77,000 within a twelve-month period. You can, however, register voluntarily and there are occasions when this can be advantageous. Your accountant should advise on this.

If you decide to set up a limited company, this will have a number issued by Companies House. You will also need to file forms naming directors, advising on shareholdings and appointing a company secretary, if needed. You will be required to file an annual return confirming or amending the information logged about the company. You must also file annual accounts in standard form, abridged for smaller companies.

Employment law

You must have formal contracts of employment with all employees. These should include:

- Remuneration and how paid

- Duties

- Holiday entitlement and how accrued

- Notice period

- Your right to summarily dismiss

Ideally you should attach a job description and details of a disciplinary procedure, setting out verbal and written warnings relating to unsatisfactory performance. The procedure must be standard for all employees.

Tax considerations

You must file annual accounts and a tax return over the internet. Your trading year can be any you choose – e.g. 1 February to the following 31 January – but the tax year runs from 6 April to the following 5 April. (It is important to note that you are not paid a salary by the business when you become self-employed. The profits belong to you and you are taxed on these. You can take 'drawings' during the year to cover living expenses but you should ensure you leave adequate funds in the business to cover taxation.) Tax is payable in two instalments, in January and July. In your first year of operation you have to pay the tax due on the first trading period plus 50 per cent on account of tax due in the current year.

If you operate through a limited company, the company is required to file a corporation tax return and pay the entire liability within nine months of the trading year end.

If you do employ personnel, you will be obliged to operate a PAYE system. HMRC issue booklets and guidance notes that you have to follow and require you to account for all payroll deductions plus the employer's National Insurance contributions.

Tax is now a swingeing charge on businesses and the community, so I will deal with the subject in some detail in the next chapter.

CHAPTER ELEVEN

Understanding Commercial Law

The moment you start a business, you are immediately subject to a plethora of rules and regulations. Most businessmen argue that there are too many, and political parties of all persuasions argue in favour of cutting red tape but never quite seem to get round to doing so. At present, as discussed in the previous chapter, you are obliged to register as self-employed and set up a direct debit so that a monthly National Insurance charge can be extracted from your bank account. Registration notifies the Inland Revenue that you have set up a business that will be subject to tax. Tax implications and structuring are dealt with later in this chapter.

As soon as you employ anybody, you are subject to further rules and regulations and, of course, health and safety legislation surrounding the work you carry out for customers. These are insurable risks. You need to take out cover for damage to third parties and/or damage caused by your product or service.

Insurance

Most people are familiar with how insurance works – certainly everyone who owns a car, and most householders. In carrying out your everyday work, you may cause damage to other people or their property. It is easy to envisage dropping something from a ladder or scaffolding that lands on somebody's head. You might work on the foundations of a semi-detached house or a party wall and in doing so damage the property next door. Insurance cover is obligatory for this type of risk, so do consult an insurance broker early and talk through the cover you need.

Professionals can also cause damage negligently. An architect could design a building that has a flawed construction and is ultimately unsafe. A lawyer could misinterpret the law applying to a particular subject and put a client to considerable expense, or assign the wrong plot of land in a property sale. Auditors could neglect to examine ownership documents and subsequently be held liable for not reporting to shareholders that the assets no longer exist. These failings too can be covered by professional indemnity insurance.

Commerce operates within a framework of law. Most of the time this is implicitly understood by the parties, but occasionally it spills over into an argument. It is as well, therefore, to understand the basic principles of the law. This is not so that you can avoid using lawyers; it is merely a broad guide to the legal implications of what you are doing.

Contract law

This impinges on every transaction. Contracts do not have to be in writing unless relating to the transfer of real estate or shares. To be valid, a contract needs only three constituents: offer, acceptance and consideration.

In simple terms, you might say to your friend: 'I will take you to the cinema tonight if you do the washing-up.' If the friend says yes, or does the washing-up, you have a binding contract that stands up in law.

Similarly somebody might say: 'How much to fix my boiler?' You reply: 'A hundred quid.' If the customer agrees, there is a binding contract. It may not have covered all aspects of what is involved – e.g. there is no commitment to repair the boiler today – but nevertheless there is an obligation on both parties. In such cases it would be implicit that the work is to be carried out within a reasonable time, but there is a potential argument about how soon is reasonable.

There can be counter-offers and extended negotiations, but the contract will only exist if the above three constituents are present. It is also self-evident that if you have spent time negotiating the conditions surrounding the offer, acceptance and consideration, you would be wise to put them in writing. However valid a verbal contract is, there is an obvious problem in that, unless witnessed, it is open to dispute as to who said what: e.g. 'You told me you would fix it on Tuesday.' 'No I didn't. I said Tuesday week.' It follows that there is less doubt about the terms agreed if the contract is in writing or can be evidenced by written documents.

You can quickly see that it pays to be disciplined and to confirm any arrangements in writing. To make this easy, you can use order acknowledgements in printed form that thank the customer for their order, and confirm price and date. This can be further improved by having your terms and conditions printed on the reverse. If you cannot set these out simply yourself, invite a solicitor to draft them for you, but try to present them in user-friendly terms, rather than 'small print' with all its implications.

Before leaving this subject, there is a further point that can be critical, relating to variations. A customer has a tradesman on site and says: 'I wonder if you could just fix that for me while you're here.' The tradesman agrees, and finds it takes him an extra day. He submits a bill, but he has a problem. The additional work was carried out with only offer and acceptance, but no 'consideration', unless in his order acknowledgement the tradesman mentioned that any additional work carried out on site would be charged at so much extra.

It is easy to slip up on small variations; it even happens with large institutions that put everything in writing. For instance, somebody is paying off a large debt to a credit card company at £50 a month and makes an offer to pay £3,000 in full and final settlement of a £10,000 debt. The credit card company writes back and says: 'We reject your offer of £3,000 and suggest £7,000 or continue paying £50 per month until the debt is extinguished.' The creditor continues paying £50 per month, seemingly ignoring the correspondence, but in fact, a new contract has been created. The credit card company has discarded its former contractual right to demand income and expenditure statements and to vary the level of repayment. Inadvertently it has made a new contract and must continue accepting £50 per month for the next seventeen years. Your printed terms and conditions should cover this type of risk.

Sale of goods

It is implicit that goods sold must be fit for purpose, regardless of whether they are guaranteed or subject to warranty. If something is purchased for the advertised or described purpose and does not fulfil that requirement, it can be returned and must be replaced or refunded.

Similarly, if you provide samples prior to sale, and the bulk of the consignment does not match the samples, the whole consignment can be rejected. In practice this tends to lead to negotiation rather than litigation. You can consent to sort the consignment and take back the inferior products or agree a discount.

Some less scrupulous businesses offer warranties and guarantees that appear to be favourable when in fact they actually limit your rights under the Sale of Goods Act. You should therefore be careful about signing such agreements.

Agency

In general terms, somebody acting as your agent does so with your full authority as regards third parties. In practice, terms of reference should be clarified in writing with your agent, making clear the situations in which he should refer back to you for guidance when acting on your behalf. If you do not like the agreement reached in your name, you should quickly write to the customer or supplier pointing out that your agent has exceeded his authority and offering to renegotiate. If they hold you to the contract, however, your only action is against your agent. In practical terms, you can start by withholding his commission and any money owing to him, or even repudiate his contract. You should have sufficient sanctions to ensure that he doesn't stray outside his brief.

In circumstances such as this, the contract should always be in writing, and it should be noted that an agent is not an employee.

Company law

A company has a separate legal identity from its owners and directors. It is governed by its memorandum and articles of association. The various Companies Acts have defined what should be contained in these documents and have included a specific example known as Table A. Most companies adopt Table A on incorporation, but variations can be introduced.

The rules cover the voting rights of various categories of shares and their entitlement to dividends; the order of repayment in the event of dissolution of the company; and the rights to participation in any surpluses. They also set out how directors should be appointed, how meetings are called, what constitutes a quorum, and the powers of directors.

Directors are appointed by shareholders to manage the company on their behalf. In small companies, the shareholders are also usually the directors but they do not have to be. The directors are empowered to commit the company contractually without incurring personal liability unless acting contrary to the wishes of the board of directors as a whole.

It is normal for the board and/or shareholders (members) to appoint a chairman and a managing director. The latter usually acts as chief executive and reports to the board, normally under a contract of employment. In small companies the chairman is generally the largest shareholder, but the chairman and directors do not have to be shareholders unless the articles oblige them to hold shares.

The annual return
Companies are obliged to file an annual return which provides details of:

- The registered office

- The number, value and classification of shares issued

- The names and addresses of directors and company secretary

- The names and addresses of every shareholder and their holdings

This is public information, which may be inspected by any interested person or body. The company is also obliged to file annual accounts within nine months of its year end in statutory form, abridged for smaller companies. This would include a balance sheet and details of turnover and profits. This too is a public document. The company file can be searched by people wanting to do business with you, such as suppliers and banks. Most of those doing so tend to use company formation agents, who are dealing daily with Companies House, to carry out a search on their behalf.

The advantages of operating through a limited company

'Limited' here is short for limited liability, i.e. your exposure is limited to the amount of capital provided to the company. You can operate your business through a limited company without putting your personal assets at risk, although, as described in Chapter Nine, banks often require additional security when lending to a company. The extra risk in such circumstances is limited to the extent of such borrowings.

Companies are taxed differently to individuals, and this fact can be used to achieve overall lower rates of tax and National Insurance if the business is structured effectively.

Business taxation

Companies are subject to corporation tax charged on annual profits. For smaller companies this currently amounts to 20 per cent on profits below £300,000 p.a. and 23 per cent above £1,500,000. There is a scale between the two figures.

Individuals receive a personal allowance of £9,440 and are subject to tax at 20 per cent on the next £32,010, when the rate goes up to 40 per cent. Employees are subject to a 12 per cent National Insurance deduction on income between £5,725 and £41,450 and an additional 2 per cent charge above £41,450 p.a. Self-employed people are subject to a 9 per cent charge between £7,755 and £41,450 and 2 per cent thereafter. The lower rate for self-employed people is due to the fact that they cannot claim unemployment benefits once they have become self-employed.

Self-employed people are able to offset certain expenses that employees are unable to claim. These include:

- Travel from their home on business if business is home-based

- Journals and newspapers

- Beverages

- Use of home as an office

- Telephone, if charged to the business

On average this typically amounts to £3,000 per year that can be offset against income. As mentioned in Chapter Ten, there is a major advantage if your spouse or partner is not already earning a separate income in that they can be paid £645, tax-free, per month for part-time assistance to your business provided they play some part, such as filing or record keeping. This further £7,740 can also be offset against your income.

By becoming self-employed you are immediately better off than a person in employment, as shown in the following calculation, based on the tax rates applying in 2013–14:

	Employed		Self-employed	
Income	£40,000	£50,000	£40,000	£50,000
Expenses			3,000	3,000
Net income			37,000	47,000
Personal all'w'ce	9,440	9,440	9,440	9,440
Taxable income	30,560	40,560	27,560	37,560
Tax at 20%	6,112	6,402	5,512	6,402
Tax at 40%		3,420		2,220
NIC	4,113	4,287	2,632	3,032
2% surcharge		171		111
Tax payable	10,225	14,280	8,144	11,765
Tax savings			2,081	2,515

Further savings of approximately £2,250 p.a. are available if you are able to employ your spouse/partner.

By operating through a company, you can achieve even better results, because you are able to pay yourself a basic salary of £7,740, which can be set against income. The company pays tax at 20 per cent on profits and can pay the balance as dividends. These are deemed to be net of tax provided your gross income does not exceed £41,450, i.e. your salary plus gross dividends.

The calculation is as follows:

Income	40,000	50,000
Expenses	3,000	3,000
Salary	7,440	7,440
	10,440	10,440
Taxable profit	29,560	39,560
Tax at 20%	5,912	7,912
Net profits	23,648	31,648
Tax saving compared with		
self-employment	2,233	3,853

Once you have an assured income above £40,000 p.a., it pays to trade through a limited company as you do save significantly on National Insurance. Your accountancy charges are likely to rise to cover the costs of handling both your own and the company's affairs, but this should only be in the region of £50 per month.

CHAPTER TWELVE

A Wide Range of Opportunities for Specialists

Professionally qualified people have always been able to launch out on their own, although in doing so, they should first study the local market and try to find a niche. Surveyors and architects could consider setting up building companies, as so many local builders are badly managed and do not provide an efficient service. House extensions, in particular, provide good opportunities; as the cost of moving has increased significantly in recent years with the imposition of taxes on purchases, many homeowners prefer to stay put. Accountants could develop management accounting services for smaller companies who cannot afford to employ full-time professionals.

As stated earlier, the consultancy field has grown significantly over the last fifty years. This has opened up opportunities for experienced managers and specialists to offer services to operating companies. I want to describe some of these in order to try and encourage more people to start businesses that use their skills and experience.

IT specialists

Many people have set up businesses in this area. It is a growing market, with opportunities in a number of areas.

Business systems

This is a wide-ranging field that covers a number of activities, such as management of an internal network where several operating managers within the company or branch operate the systems that relate to their particular function, forming part of a wider whole. Some specialists will be programmers capable of devising and/or extending specific systems to meet a need. Others will manage and maintain systems. Most will have a window on the world and awareness of developments taking place within the IT industry.

Once more you need to determine what you are and where you fit in as a specialist, as well as how you could carry out a wider brief and what you can offer the market. Initially it is not unreasonable to suggest that virtually all businesses now use IT to a greater or lesser extent, but this is too general. Again, in viewing the overall market you need to think in terms of what you can offer as a specific product or project, bearing in mind that you are not looking for a full-time job or seeking to replace existing personnel employed by the client company.

You must also think in terms of what benefits you can bring to the client's business. This is a fundamental question that applies to people of all disciplines. If the project you are proposing does not help the client to increase his sales, improve his service or bring about economies, it begs the question as to why he should want to employ you.

Let us begin by considering why IT has gained such wide acceptance in a variety of businesses of all sizes and types.

Streamlining systems

The principal objective of every business is to find and serve customers by providing a product or service.

Most businesses have a marketing operation that is concerned with promoting its product or service to customers and trying to ensure it does so as efficiently as possible. They also have to produce or buy products and find a means of distributing their product or service efficiently to their customers. They must then coordinate these activities through administrative systems and ensure that they charge for products or services and meet the costs of producing or providing them.

In small businesses starting out, the owner manager carries out all of these functions, but as the business grows, it tends to add management roles concerned with:

- Marketing, sales and customer communications

- Production or management of the service

- Central planning, coordination and buying

- Accounting

- Personnel management or human relations

Typically a business will have grown to perhaps £10 million turnover and/or 200–300 employees before deploying managers in all of these functions, each with systems that help them understand what is going on in their department and acting or reacting accordingly. Thus most businesses of any size might have five separate systems, each requiring maintenance of records. This has provided fertile ground for the computer and IT systems industry.

Computer storage and maintenance of individual systems has led to large clerical savings, and the progressive integration of departmental systems into company systems has provided further economies and clearer overviews that help management and decision-taking. In simple terms, the IT industry and its disciplines have brought about streamlining and more efficient operations of business systems. These days, a range of 'off-the-shelf' software packages are available for both general and specific industry use, while larger companies deploy leading management consultants to work at the frontiers of information technology, creating bespoke systems that provide greater efficiency and economies.

This background picture suggests that few opportunities exist for solo consultants, but openings could occur in the smaller, growing companies. Such opportunities could present themselves in any sector of industry, so it might be that the target market should be defined by size rather than industry grouping, although it would be wise, at least initially, to approach the type of companies where you have experience.

Possible product services

Since software systems already exist, an obvious service to expanding companies would involve making an initial study of the client's existing business and suggesting what off-the-shelf system might be deployed either to facilitate expansion or to effect economies. It is immediately obvious that this is a one-off project, lasting perhaps two days a month for three to six months. You could present a report outlining present systems in use by the business and describing how available IT systems could be deployed to advantage. If the report is acceptable, you could offer to help with installation and training.

This type of approach is attractive both to you and to the client. It is highly probable that in many companies systems have grown haphazardly and even the managing director is sometimes unaware of what is being done and why. The focus of most managing directors in smaller businesses is usually the product and its technology or sales – quite often both, particularly if the MD founded the business. They are rarely all-round administrators and are quite often frustrated about constant administrative problems but do not want to employ extra people merely to deal with them. This in itself is an opportunity. The offer of two days a week with a definite time limit is very attractive compared with hiring full-time personnel, and streamlining administration has obvious benefits.

If you carry out this project successfully, you might be contacted at a future date to advise on other aspects of systems development, and could secure repeat business. Alternatively you might suggest a retainer for one day a month to keep an eye on things as the systems guru.

The big advantage for you is that you can write, say, £1,000 a week income into your forward plan for the next few months, and perhaps £500 per month thereafter. The time commitment is not onerous and you can see that with as few as three clients you could earn in the order of £3,000 a week. Life, of course, is never quite as simple as this, as you need to find more business to follow through when these projects end, but nevertheless, with perhaps 20–30 clients acquired over two to three years, you could achieve a six-figure income, which places you in the top 2–3 per cent income earners in the UK.

I would encourage all IT specialists to think in terms of expanding your horizons to consider wider issues about how IT is used in business. Understanding your customer is a fundamental requirement for anybody who wishes to succeed in business. This is a particularly fertile field, with a very large market.

There is a serious opportunity to build a solid business by providing a systems review and maintenance business to smaller growing companies.

Training

Young people today grow up with computers and take them for granted. Younger managers have become accustomed to them and adapted them for their own use, but many people still lack computer skills. The majority of people in the country are able to use less than 10 per cent of possible computer applications. A large number would welcome further training, but price is likely to be an issue. This is also a difficult market to approach cost-effectively.

A training service could be offered to companies, but it would need to relate to internal systems, which would require a study of the systems and software used by the company and an analysis of operator skills. This is unlikely to produce a clear-cut result showing obvious needs, unless it coincided with a new installation. Logically, such training should form part of the systems review project described above.

Mobile phone technology is also moving extremely rapidly, with phones starting to replace computers in many instances. This should prove another lucrative area for IT specialists, but will also need to form part of a total business approach as described above.

HR/personnel managers

HR covers a wide area of functions, and yet most small companies do not employ HR managers until they have grown to employ in excess of one hundred personnel. Many companies with fewer than a hundred employees do not have a full-time person responsible for this function. Clearly a market exists for people with HR skills who want to use them to build a business of their own. In most large companies the role covers recruitment, management development and training, job evaluation, personnel record maintenance, negotiations with trade unions, labour relationships and disciplinary procedures. These are important policy areas that often require specialists in each.

Recruitment

Virtually every business has constant staff turnover and the need to engage and/or replace people. This can be a time-consuming exercise, particularly for companies seeking employees with particular skills. They also need compatible people who will fit into teams and work diligently, so some preliminary assessment is usually needed. In small companies the managing director probably handles this task along with everything else, or it might be dealt with by the manager in charge of a department such as production or administration. As businesses grow, they tend to use outside sources to handle these requirements.

Staff bureaux

You will find these in most towns, usually in high-street premises where they can be noticed by passers-by. If you are looking for a job, you can drop in and register and be considered for any opportunities currently available. Such places make themselves known to the business community by mailing local companies. They charge a fee, usually in the range of 10–15 per cent of the job's basic annual salary, and provide the client with a CV and a brief background for each applicant. General labourers or unskilled personnel are put forward with little or no supporting documentation.

These are reasonably simple businesses to establish, requiring little capital investment other than renting and furnishing an office, almost certainly less than £10,000. They are relatively easy to build up, subject to the amount of local competition. A particular advantage of this type of business is that it can be systematised – for taking on additional recruiters, if the demand is there, or for setting up further offices in adjacent towns. Such a business could generate a significant income within a few years, possibly close to six figures, although it is difficult to defend against new competitors if the local market is fairly static.

Management recruitment

This is a more limited opportunity, but probably more lucrative. These agencies charge fees of between 15 and 25 per cent of first-year salaries. You could, therefore, earn a high income even if you only made one placement per month. This is easier said than done, however, as competition is tough. Entry into this market would be through focusing on two or three industry sectors that you have good knowledge of, or alternatively by concentrating on particular jobs like

IT specialists or accountants. To succeed, you would need to build relationships with company chairmen and chief executives to create a client base of fifty or more companies that are likely to use your services.

This type of business requires more investment than staff bureaux, as you would need a suite of offices, tastefully furnished and with private interview rooms. You would also need a substantial PR and entertainment budget, since high-level contacts are essential if you want to succeed. You would have to recruit reception and secretarial staff, as national advertising for senior positions can often bring in several hundred applications that need reading and some response, even if only a postcard. Appointments for interviews need to be arranged and notes made on each candidate seen, with a final shortlist prepared for interviews by the client. This needs a background report for each client with CV attached in a consistent format. Detailed accounting records are also required, with the costs of advertising allocated to the relevant client, and most recruiters charge stage payments as the process sometimes takes several months from the original brief to final appointment.

Head-hunting

This type of consultant is usually an ex senior manager of main board status, since head-hunters are not employed to find anyone below managing director or senior group manager level. The rewards are high; head-hunters rarely work for less than 30 per cent of first-year salary and generally handle appointments with incomes over £100,000 p.a. This is very much contact work, involving speaking to people in the industry sector to establish who might be likely candidates and then approaching such people individually.

There is then an initial meeting for a discussion, followed by an in-depth interview of the most likely candidates before reports are prepared for the client.

International head-hunters tend to have offices in several countries, but quite a few, working predominantly within the UK, operate from their homes or possibly one small office, probably in London, although location is rarely a critical factor.

This service could be an add-on for a successful management recruitment agency, but quite a few head-hunters work alone. This business is hard to enter without a good track record at senior management level, but is not exclusive to people from a personnel management background. Senior managers from other disciplines, particularly ex managing directors with good contacts, have become successful in this field.

Organisation structuring and job evaluation services

This type of service should be aimed at slightly larger growing businesses that have probably not yet created their own HR department. Rapid growth often brings a trail of people problems in its wake, particularly if attributable to mergers or acquisition of other businesses. Opportunities, though limited, are likely to last for several months and fees can be charged at fairly high rates, possibly in excess of £500 per day. If successful, initial involvement should lead to an ongoing relationship with the client company.

Having experienced one or two mergers during my career, I have been surprised by the effect they can have on staff morale and on the performance of individual managers. Some seemingly capable people find themselves out of their depth when the business suddenly expands by over

50 per cent in a matter of months, uncertain about the management systems and procedures that are changing around them. Total re-evaluation of roles becomes inevitable and the need for organisational changes is glaringly obvious.

Ascertaining who fits where in a management structure is best handled by a dispassionate outside specialist who allows the individuals to speak frankly about how they see problems inside the company, what they believe their job is about and where they feel they need help to perform effectively. This is likely to apply at all management levels. The underlying objective is, of course, to determine what the company needs by way of personnel to staff the business adequately and, thereafter, define how existing people match the job specifications that emerge. This should inevitably lead to the creation of a remuneration policy with appropriate pay scales that are in line with the industry sector and local rates. It is also likely that, in carrying out this exercise, you will identify training needs.

This type of project needs people with communication skills of a high level and should ideally be carried out, say, three days per week for a few months. It is a wide-ranging project that is not easy to sell, and you will therefore need several progress meetings with the managing and other directors to ensure that the conclusions that emerge will be supported and that the resultant structure will be an interdependent team committed to the success of the business.

Such projects are rewarding both financially and professionally. However, they occur less frequently than other types of project, so you will probably need another string to your bow. The personnel field offers a wide range of opportunities.

Training services

This too is a potentially wide area with several options. You could offer a bespoke service to companies, specialising in a few sectors, probably aimed at businesses in the £5–25 million turnover range, as it tends to be larger companies that specifically employ training managers. This approach would be best handled by compiling a database of such companies and progressively making contact with individual managing directors to discuss a programme to identify training needs, followed by recommendations about how to meet such needs and, of course, the benefits that would be derived. It might be helpful to create an image to promote this type of service, possibly sending out mailshots that describe you and your achievements, with supporting case histories.

Training is usually on a list of subjects managing directors think they ought to do something about, but it often slips their mind, as other matters tend to take greater priority. It is, nevertheless, something that can help boost morale, since it makes staff believe that they work for a caring company that is interested in them as individuals. Indeed, this should be one of your sales points.

The range of possible training is quite wide: specific technical skills necessary to do a particular job; sales training, which is always popular; management training in basic skills and communication processes – a problem in many companies. A general assessment, however, is a good place to start, and might take one to four weeks according to the size of the company. The subsequent report might indicate areas for you to carry out internal training sessions or recommend outside courses for specific individuals.

Providing training courses

Such courses tend to be specialist, but this is an area where reputation is important and, once established, can lead on to a well-remunerated career. To be effective, you will need to invest in advertising and PR in order to promote courses, and meeting places at which to stage them. Be aware, however, that the response rate is somewhat unpredictable.

Some of the most successful trainers are experts in their particular field. Sales gurus often attract several hundred respondents to presentations in large hotels and charge several hundred pounds to each. Financial specialists charge sometimes a couple of thousand pounds and attract an audience of close to a hundred. It can be a profitable business for such people, who can generate £100,000 in attendance fees for an outlay of less than 25 per cent of that sum. They probably only do two or three performances a year and usually back them up with consultancy services to large companies that also command high fees. I have often thought about running training courses about self-employment.

> **This type of business is not restricted to specialist training or personnel managers.**

Promoting the service

For specialists, the writing of a book on their subject, followed by a series of successful, well-advertised presentations around the country, is, of course, a clever way to build a consultancy-type business. You create a reputation that helps attract clients and opportunities to present. It has been used by people from many walks of life, particularly in sales, marketing and finance.

An ongoing need

The traditional management training courses are still of value, particularly for smaller companies who recognise a need but do not have the internal facilities. These types of courses can be standardised as one- or two-day sessions in various towns around the country, and be promoted to businesses in the locality. Ideally they should include a blend of short lectures and case studies to ensure participant involvement. They can be run in local hotels and aimed at as few as twenty participants, who pay up to £1,000 per day to attend. The costs of staging could be budgeted at barely 10 per cent of fee income. By running as few as six courses per annum, you could generate a six-figure income.

Employee contracts and personnel policies

This is, I believe, a major opportunity area for former HR managers, and one that could be structured as a franchise or network for the more ambitious, as it is relatively easy to systematise and sell to smaller companies that are often unaware of the legal implications of employing people. A surprisingly large number of such companies finish up in front of tribunals, which hand down hefty damages for wrongful dismissals that sometimes bankrupt the business.

Most businesses are started by individuals with a specialist skill that they believe they can deploy to generate an income. A high proportion of such individuals are not rounded or even experienced managers, but nevertheless go on to drive the business forward. In doing so, they expand it to a point where they need to employ people to carry out mundane jobs and share some of the growing workload. The company structures are rarely pre-planned, but evolve to meet particular problems at a point in time. Consequently mistakes are sometimes made. A person recruited to meet a specific need turns out subsequently to have no ongoing role in the business, so the boss fires them. That is when his problems begin, because he did so without warning and in breach of a contract that failed to deal with the wider issue of the employee's implied terms of employment.

> **I**n simple terms, a high proportion of smaller business owner-managers do not understand the legal implications of employment contracts and disciplinary procedures. What a marvellous opportunity for people who do!

If this were my business, I would create a database of 5,000 companies and send out mailshots emphasising the risks of being hauled up before a tribunal and punished for breach of contract, then explaining how I could solve the problem for them. I would probably include a covering letter, personally addressed to the managing directors of, say, fifty companies per month. The letter would indicate that I would telephone each of them in the near future to make an appointment.

In the subsequent meeting, I would offer to review all employees' terms of contract and revise them in a manner that complied with legislation, setting out hours of work, holiday entitlement and period of notice, with reference to the company's personnel policies and disciplinary procedures. This would be supported by the production of a booklet that set out the rules. These would, of course, be in standard form so that the booklet could simply be customised for each client. Such books could be printed on demand for less than a couple of pounds each. The whole project could probably be carried out in less than a week and sold for up to a couple of thousand pounds.

This is potentially a classic case whereby a virtually standard product can be adapted for almost any client and sold on a fear basis, almost always a more compelling concept than reward. It could, of course, be married to other services and made part of a wider package.

> **This is not only an opportunity for personnel managers. It could be handled by an experienced manager from almost any discipline.**

Designers

Design covers an extremely wide field. It features strongly in the advertising world and has an impact on virtually every type of finished product and its packaging, particularly for retail products. Over the years I have met a few people who have created and built significant businesses as designers in various fields. Some have suffered from a lack of commercial awareness, and possibly allow too much freedom for their creative ideas at the expense of empathising with clients and working to a budget. In many situations designers are less concerned with costs, particularly in the initial stages, than in generating ideas, which is fine provided they think about cost later.

There are some fields of design where it is difficult to succeed as a self-employed solo operator, such as fashion design, where concepts are presented at major events, costing tens of thousands to stage and backed by heavy PR activity. There are, nevertheless, many opportunities that I want to discuss, under three basic headings.

Graphic design

For the most part, graphic design is associated with marketing activity. There are many graphic design businesses operating today, however, who secure business directly from clients as well as acting as a subcontractor for advertising agencies and occasionally for printers, who are frequently asked to come up with something original.

Like all start-up businesses of whatever nature, you do have to go out and secure some business. In doing so, you are looking initially at a large and diverse market, so you need to choose specific areas, based on former experience and/or particular skills. Random approaches and mailshots are too general and ultimately time-consuming. You need to create a database of best prospects – a concept I have repeatedly referred to as the most effective way for solo practitioners to identify possible clients and make direct approaches. This type of identification also allows you to do some research and find out what prospective clients sell, and what sales aids they use – catalogues, newsletters, leaflets, etc.

Design your own sales aids

As a graphic designer, you ought to produce at least a folded card pamphlet/brochure that fits easily into a standard envelope. It need not be expensive but should reflect the skills you are promoting, as well as providing a background story about you and your achievements. This could be sent to managing directors of prospective clients with a personally addressed covering letter, of no more than three paragraphs, seeking an appointment to discuss company advertisements and literature. A follow-up phone call is essential.

A further possible approach is to obtain copies of a company's current literature and write a short, but polite, critique suggesting how you could help improve it. This may upset some people, but others could be provoked into positive action, in which case you are virtually certain to win some business.

Some less common opportunities

It is worth considering the market carefully and thinking about the types of business that advertise regularly. Management recruitment agencies, for instance, might place £5,000 advertisements from time to time in national newspapers. This could be steadily repeating business: laying out the advert to meet the paper's criteria and ensuring that it stands out. A certain amount of contact with local printers could have some spin-offs, and, of course, working alongside advertising agencies, who need designers from time to time, could be lucrative. Pricing will probably be based on hourly rates for time spent, plus materials at cost with a handling charge added. In addition, commission can be earned on advertisements placed.

Package designers

This is an interesting field of activity that combines an element of both technical and creative design; in some cases, the packaging is integral to the product or the manner in which it is used. This is particularly true in the cosmetics industry, where applicators or sprays are part of the basic container. In most industries that sell products through retailers, the packaging has to protect the product as well as present it in an attractive manner on the shelves.

The number of companies likely to be involved in this type of creative packaging is almost certainly fewer than

250 throughout the UK, so finding out who they are is not an onerous task. It is also fairly certain that they will be open to approaches from creative designers; their businesses depend on such people.

On the face of it, this is a relatively small market, but one where change is constant and design critical to success. Wherever change is taking place, opportunities exist. A successful business could be built with as few as three or four clients in this area, although for security reasons you would want to extend your customer base.

A small database could quickly be established and used in similar fashion to the methods advocated in earlier sections. In this area, however, I believe a bold approach of direct telephone contact would quickly pay off, especially if you have a track record or designs for a product in the market you are able to point to.

Pricing policy could be varied. The worth of a creative design is an open question. You could charge on a time-related basis, plus materials, but how much thinking time could you truly attribute to a particular design? You could ask for royalties, but the client might prefer an alternative design subsequently and you cannot be sure he will go ahead with your proposal. Ideally you will ask for an exclusive brief to put forward initial ideas, and then work up two or three full samples for a final selection. You should produce a final specification in cooperation with chosen packaging suppliers.

You could prepare quotations to carry out the brief at a high hourly rate, say not less than £100, and ask for stage payments. If you could structure a retainer to produce three special packages a year for a couple of clients, you would probably be working at close to full capacity.

Product design

There is an element of design in virtually every product conceived, but from a self-employed designer's point of view, much of this has to be taken for granted. You are unlikely to find opportunities to redesign a bar of soap or the shape of a biscuit. These products are changed from time to time, but usually in house and by employees with a depth of knowledge about the products. Involvement in such activities does therefore require industry focus. Even then, with traditional and/or long-established products, it is more a question of being in the right place at the right time, rather than something that will be brought about by your own initiative. It follows that you have no control over your business if working in such an environment.

Conceptual thinking is of vital importance within the economy as a whole, but viewed as an employment opportunity, you will need to think the entire concept through from creation of a prototype to its place in the market.

Concentrate on a few industry sectors

The situation you face is similar to that of package designers. You need to be able to think laterally in relation to materials used in manufacture and how the product is used and presented to the market. This is likely to restrict you to fewer industries and probably oblige you to confine yourself to only one. Even so, considerable fortunes can be made with this type of activity.

Research and development departments are a feature of most modern businesses. This includes keeping abreast of new technologies and changes within the industry, and process developments and small modifications to products to lower production costs. The self-employed designer needs to focus on industries where change is constant:

- Fashion design and clothing

- Gifts and souvenirs

- Toys

- Board games

- Toiletries

- Cosmetics

- Wallpaper

- Textiles

- Furniture

Most of these industries rely heavily on introducing new products, sometimes only marginally different from older ones. They usually have trade fairs to show their new ideas to the retail trade and exporters and import agents, and take advance orders with promises of delivery in time for new seasons, peak sale times, etc. They have their own internal designers and marketing departments planning product launches and so forth, but most welcome fresh ideas. They are all looking for that new trend to boost sales.

These industries have much in common, but even so, you are unlikely to be a toy inventor, wallpaper designer and furniture maker all at the same time. You need to define your own skills and strengths and identify the industries that are most likely to use them. Your previous experience will also be a guide. You then need to study the market. In this respect it is worthwhile contacting the Institute of Marketing, who have market reports on most UK industries. These will enable you to focus on the main companies in the trade, their range of products and scale of operation.

Identifying and approaching your market

Having established who the main players are, you can study their websites and identify key personnel to contact. If your timing is right, you should visit their stands at trade fairs and make personal contacts. With a little dedication you could build your own industry dossier within a few weeks and start thinking about the product ranges and how you could contribute to prospective clients' businesses.

Copyright belongs to you

You have copyright in design and therefore some automatic protection against plagiarism when you reveal your ideas. Patent application is available but enormously expensive when you contemplate world markets. A feature of most of the industries under consideration here, however, is that if your client likes the idea, he will want to bring it to market as quickly as possible. This being the case, you can tie up patent protection as part of negotiating a licence once all parties are confident of some product longevity.

You do have ownership of the product and, with something worthwhile, should be able to negotiate an upfront fee and royalty on sales, usually 5 per cent, and enforce a minimum annual royalty. Many designers in these fields of activity have ownership of several products and/or designs that generate substantial royalties. You would be lucky, however, to enjoy ongoing royalties beyond five years due to the nature of the business. Every now and then a new product becomes an established brand or generic term and goes on for a lifetime – think of Scrabble and Monopoly, for instance.

Other possibilities

I have dealt at length with the above management skills to show how such skills and experience can be deployed to build a one-person business. I have chosen these because they are quite wide-ranging, and to show that businesses can be set up based on a function that normally fits into a wider framework. The essential point is to find a niche and exploit it. You can bring wider skills to bear once you have established client relationships. The same logic can be applied to many other management roles, as shown in the following subsections.

General managers

People with this experience could focus on their core skills, but could also choose to provide counselling services to senior executives, operating as a form of alter ego for a couple of days a month. This is an opportunity area that is growing in popularity. Established counsellors are commanding fees in the order of £1,000 a day.

A further option is to provide strategic planning services to growing businesses. This would initially be based on establishing the strengths and weaknesses of the business, compared with competitors and in relation to the market as a whole. Clearly this would force a major debate within the company, leading to a series of action plans and a consideration of strategic options for the business. This, too, could ultimately become a lucrative practice.

Marketing managers

The above options could also be developed by senior marketing managers. In addition they could consider starting advertising agencies, if they have sufficient resources and good contacts. Strategic marketing services could be developed in similar fashion to business strategy, described above. This could also include brand positioning and development.

Both marketing and general managers could offer their services as non-executive directors and ultimately sit on the boards of several companies.

Buyers

Your expertise could be valuable to smaller businesses that lack the skills and systems. The selected market would have to be companies who purchase probably in excess of £500,000 a year, where you might be able to show ongoing savings of £50,000 to justify involvement with the client. Again, this could be sold as an initial project, but you could lock yourself in to a subsequent day or two a month to monitor progress and ensure the system is followed.

Engineers

This is another wide-ranging area that might cover production, mechanical, electrical and maintenance engineering. Selected services could be applied primarily to manufacturing companies. You could, for instance, look at the production line and show where significant efficiencies could be achieved by using alternative equipment, removing bottlenecks or improving staffing arrangements. Planning maintenance systems could be installed to reduce the risk of total breakdowns and the idle time costs that ensue.

Bank managers

Many business owners do not really understand finance or how to raise it. This implies that a large market is available for people who do. Bank managers probably see more business plans than anybody else and so are in a position to offer this service and help clients to raise finance. Equally importantly, they should be able to pinpoint companies that will be unable to increase borrowings and to point out why.

This type of service would allow you to work alongside clients on an occasional basis, charging fees, to monitor progress and help bring them to a position where they would have an improved chance of securing appropriate finance. You could agree small percentages on funds raised.

Others

I cannot possibly cover everything in this chapter. There are some quite significant omissions, such as production managers, quality controllers and property managers, all of whom have skills that could be offered on a part-time basis. I have, however, described in general terms how to build a business on the skills and experience you possess, and have given several examples of how these skills can be adapted and promoted to create income-generating opportunities. Anyone can do it.

> **You need to do some lateral thinking and use your imagination, believe in yourself and start talking to people.**

CHAPTER THIRTEEN
Internet Businesses

Using the internet
During the last twenty years, the internet has grown to become one of the most important business vehicles in the world. It is a source of both information and misinformation, but also a brilliant means of communicating at low cost.

A huge number of people have already exploited this new opportunity and created successful businesses. Many have seized on the chance to present themselves as gurus in a variety of fields and offer training courses on business ideas, internet marketing, trading, fitness, health and diet. Meanwhile, mail-order companies invite all their potential clients to disclose their email addresses, enabling the companies to communicate more immediately and to use websites rather than printed catalogues as a means of describing their products.

Some businesses owe their existence to the internet. They have their origins in different practices but have grown enormously through use of the internet, and continue to do so.

Internet businesses available
There are hundreds of business ideas being offered that can be operated with a modest amount of investment and

training and are capable of generating additional income either on a part-time or full-time basis. Many of them claim that if you follow the advice offered, you will make a fortune in ten minutes a day while sitting on the beach. It's a lovely idea, probably aimed at the gullible. In any business you need to acquire certain skills and determine how best to use your time in the most productive and beneficial manner.

I think it is probably true that the internet has opened up a wide variety of business opportunities, many of which are new concepts. In other cases it has aided existing businesses to capitalise on wider communication opportunities and helped to lower costs. It has also created new lifestyle opportunities for one-person businesses.

It is also undoubtedly true that if your entire business is conducted over the internet, it doesn't matter where you are located. You may well be able to prod things along by spending only an hour a day on your computer and still be aware of any developments taking place. You could certainly choose to live in the sun and operate a wide variety of internet businesses.

Research is necessary

I would encourage any redundant manager to look seriously at the internet and consider any available opportunities, but to cross-check what other people are saying about them before investing or subscribing. The potential is enormous. It has already changed the nature of retail, home selling and mail order quite dramatically, and will continue to do so. Equally important is that you can be immediately in touch with international markets and communicate with people all over the planet. This clearly helps to enhance trade and creates enormous markets for new ideas, but be sure to think things through before launching out.

In this section I am dealing with the subject under three headings:

- **Financial trading:** I have taken a hard look at this and misspent a significant amount of money, without success. Nevertheless, it is an area of activity where money can be made

- **Auctions:** I have looked quite closely at this subject but I have no practical experience. Some people, however, have built successful businesses or developed a good part-time income

- **Internet marketing:** I have launched a new company in this field concerned with information publishing but am conscious that there is still a great deal to learn

Financial trading

There are three main categories of trading, each with several sub-markets. Foreign exchange, generally known as FOREX, is by far the biggest. The total value of transactions runs to in excess of a trillion pounds daily on the main exchanges throughout the world. The second major area is trading in stocks and shares, which again can be carried out globally. The third is commodity trading.

Historically these activities have been carried out by specialist brokers – foreign exchange dealers, stockbrokers and commodity brokers – who have direct access to the market makers on the exchanges. Investors would usually hold a portfolio of stocks or commodities and would issue buy or sell requests to brokers, who would execute the deal within seconds and confirm with a bought or sold note. In practice, most investors were buying on the expectation or hope that prices would rise so that they could eventually sell and show a profit. Brokers made a small commission on the deal and the government collected stamp duty.

Dealing in stocks and shares and holding a portfolio was perceived as a rich person's part-time occupation, but also as gambling, in that it was implicit that if somebody made money, somebody else lost it. This was particularly true of foreign currency. The underlying value of shares could rise as companies expanded, and commodity trading was more susceptible to supply and demand, with markets affected by poor or abundant harvests.

Spread betting

This concept has emerged within the last thirty years or so, but has seen enormous growth due to the internet. IG Index was the first company to enter the market, and has been followed by several others. These companies show the latest prices for virtually every share, commodity and currency traded on recognised markets/exchanges. In practice they are slightly behind the market but allow trading on the prices shown. Prices for shares are shown to two decimal places. Punters bet on the movement, but are able to buy on the expectation of prices rising (the technical term is 'long') or sell with the expectation of prices falling, when they would buy to close the deal ('short'). The spread-betting company takes a small margin between the buy and sell prices so is unaffected by market movements.

Using charts

In order to trade, you must open an account and deposit funds. Your account grows or falls according to how successfully you trade. The spread-betting companies usually provide a charting service so that you can see at a glance what has been happening to prices. The charts can be set to show a price movement every five minutes, or in hours or days, enabling you to judge long- and short-term trends or to see patterns, highs and lows.

A pattern is established whereby the price bounces off the ceiling. This can be taken as an indicator that every time the price rises to such a ceiling, it will fall back again. This is perceived as a 'sell' signal. Conversely, if it hits a low three times and immediately starts to climb, it is treated as a 'buy' signal. It is apparent that the price is fluctuating within a channel so you buy at the bottom and sell at the top.

There are trading experts all over the internet who claim to have systems that will tell you the selling point or buying point by reference to patterns on the charts. It is also possible to superimpose other readings on the charts, such as the moving average price over a period, the volume of trading and other mathematical readings.

In order to trade, you call up a share or currency pair, open a deal ticket, and set a stop loss, i.e. if the price moves say twenty points in the opposite direction to your prognosis, you are taken out automatically at a pre-fixed loss. You set a price, say £1 a point movement, then click on buy or sell. The trade is instantly confirmed, and continuously reflects on screen how much you are winning or losing until you close the deal. It's all quite exciting because prices are constantly moving. Transactions are usually closed at the spread-betting company's close of business, though you can pay a small charge to have them carried over. However, these charges can be significant if you are thinking of running the deal for a few weeks or months.

FOREX

With FOREX trading you are normally betting on a change in one currency compared with another. GBP/USD, for instance, denotes the pound against the US dollar, currently around $1.5500 to £1. The rates are always extended to four decimal places. You bet on movements of the fourth place. The market shows a buying and a selling price, known as the spread. If you trade long, expecting the value of the pound to increase against the dollar, then you might buy at 1.5502 with the selling price at 1.5498. You will show an immediate loss of four points, usually referred to as pips. You must wait until the selling price exceeds 1.6002 before you are showing a profit.

Using a stop loss

Most investors set a stop loss when entering a deal. This limits the amount you can lose if the market moves against you. There is, however, no limit on the upside, so in theory, you limit the loss to a maximum sum you can afford.

Markets, however, are volatile, so whilst the pound could rise quickly, showing a profit, it could also turn sharply against you. This can be countered by moving the stop loss. Assuming you set your initial stop loss at twenty points, or 1.5978, and the selling price moves to 1.6022, you are now twenty pips up. If the price rises further, you can move your stop loss to 1.6002, creating a situation whereby you cannot lose. You could also sell half of your holding so that you lock in a profit and move the stop loss to 1.6002 to prevent you from any loss on the remainder. As the price continues to rise, you move your stop loss up again, perhaps to within ten pips of the latest price, thereby locking in a further profit whatever happens. This technique is known as a 'trailing stop loss'.

Calculating risk

Most pundits recommend that you limit your potential loss to a maximum of 2 per cent of your available funds or kitty. Some are even more conservative. The effect of this is that if you have put up £1,000 with the spread-betting company, you can only risk £20 per deal.

On the above example, if you are betting £1 per pip, you would set your stop loss at £20, or 1.5982. This means that if the selling price drops to this level, you are automatically taken out of the transaction at that price and you have lost £20. If your kitty drops, you can afford less than a twenty-pip stop loss or must lower the price per pip to, say, 95 pence. Conversely you can increase as you move ahead.

A very fast market

Prices are changing constantly in this market and can swing by twenty pips in a matter of seconds and reverse immediately, so it takes nerves of steel to play for high stakes, and fairly constant attention to the market. Professional traders like volatility and tend to play for set periods, say between 8 and 10 a.m. and then again between 1 and 3 p.m., when the US market is at its busiest. Most professionals make few trades and pick their moment. They also set themselves objectives for the day, e.g. a profit of fifty pips, and then withdraw from the market. A fifty-pip gain every day would make you quite rich in time. A fundamental principle, however, is never to play with money you cannot afford to lose.

Betting systems

The internet is awash with people selling systems. The reality is that few of them work and none of them work all the time. In fairness, most systems purveyors admit that nothing is perfect, but by managing your deals within the framework described above and operating a trailing stop loss, you can move the odds more in your favour.

Most systems look for patterns on the charts. Triangles, channels and flags on an upward or downward trend are the most commonly used. An ascending triangle occurs when the upward trend is broken by a downward drift before climbing to its previous high, then falling again more slowly and reversing before hitting the previous low. You should be able to draw a horizontal line across the peaks with a further line linking the recent lows meeting the horizontal. A breakout occurs when the price moves above the horizontal. This is deemed to be a continuation of the upward trend and a signal to buy. Descending triangles are merely the reverse of the above.

Symmetrical channels occur when the peaks and troughs are progressively lower so that you can draw triangles linking lows and highs that meet. When the pattern is broken by a move outside the triangle in the direction of the previous trend, this is a signal to buy on an upward trend or sell on a downward one. Channels are parallel lines before a breakout in the previous direction. Flags are a channel in the opposite direction to the trend before the breakout signal occurs.

As a personal observation, I have found it difficult to identify these signals with any real consistency.

Support and resistance

This concept is easier to predict, and provides what are known as scalping opportunities, i.e. chances to capture small profits.

Imagine that an upward trend is showing on the chart and climbs to a previous peak that was achieved some time earlier, before falling back again. If this pattern occurs three times and you are able to draw a horizontal line across the peaks, this clearly shows that there is price resistance at this level and the sellers pull out. The market has determined a ceiling. This is an opportunity to sell or go short. Unfortunately, there is no guide as to how far the market will drop back before climbing to this ceiling again, but small profits could be available, say ten or fifteen pips within a short space of time.

Support is the opposite of resistance, and is where a floor is determined by the low points occurring at the same price, presenting opportunities to buy on a retreat from the floor.

> There is no certainty that these floors and ceilings will remain in place. They rarely last more than a day or so, and frequently less.

Stocks and shares

Most Western countries have stock markets on which the major companies are listed; hence you can buy shares on the Johannesburg or Toronto stock exchanges as well as in London or New York. Some international businesses are listed on several exchanges.

When you buy shares in companies, there is an underlying product. You do actually own the shares, and provided you hold on to them long enough, you will be listed as a shareholder by the company. This entitles you to receive reports and dividends when paid, and enables you to find out a great deal about the company you have invested in.

Historically most companies became listed with a view to raising money on the exchange, and they are obliged to follow strict rules about disclosure of dealings in shares by directors, notification of results and timetables, etc. Even so, there is often volatility in share prices as quoted by the market, and they are frequently at variance with underlying values.

Spread betting

This method of dealing is available with stocks and shares as well as FOREX. In this case, however, you are not betting on one currency against another, merely on how the price changes on the open market. The rules are the same as with FOREX: you are betting on penny or one cent movements at a price per penny up or down. The same guidelines apply. You should decide a stop loss and a maximum potential loss per transaction. You can study the charts and apply similar types of systems as described above, and close or open deals instantly.

> **S**pread betting is a form of gambling, and as such, profits are not subject to either income tax or capital gains tax.

Auctions

There are several auction sites on the internet, but eBay is by far the most popular, with thousands of people using the medium to conduct a full-time business. It probably started as a vehicle to sell the occasional artefact that was no longer wanted or needed, but has seen exponential growth. Several hundreds of millions of dollars now change hands every year.

Find a product source

If you wish to build a serious business through eBay and/ or other auction sites, you need to become knowledgeable about the types of products you intend to sell. You have to be able to buy cheap and sell at a profit. Profits are not guaranteed, but effective buying helps to keep the probability in your favour. It follows that you need to study what sells consistently at auction, and the prices being realised, and to find a source of supply that provides you with your product at a cost well below the likely market price. You also want an active market in the items you are contemplating selling.

You are not necessarily looking for expensive products; ideally you should focus on things that people collect. This might include out-of-print books by recognised authors, or nineteenth-century photographs of town centres. These types of products can be acquired for a few pounds and are often fought over at auctions, yielding profits at a few multiples of cost price.

Presenting the product

Nowadays it is normal to show a photograph of the product, so it is obviously necessary to make sure it is clean and displayed to best effect, with an unobtrusive background. A brief description should be added and, where appropriate, any information available relating to provenance.

Pricing guidelines

Experts differ about the use of setting a reserve price. It helps to ensure you avoid losses, but also hints to the market that the product is worth little more than the reserve indicated, so bidding might tail off. The balance of the argument probably calls for a reserve price on expensive or rare products where you expect keen interest.

A similar diversity of opinion exists about showing the count of the number of visitors to the site, with some pundits claiming that while rising numbers show a keen interest, it can work against you if there is little interest.

Apart from these factors, you have little influence on the auction other than ensuring that the presentation is attractive and the narrative helps promote the product.

Delivery and customer contact

It is your responsibility as the seller to ensure that the product arrives safely with the customer. This implies that you must think about transit packaging and means of delivery.

It is self-evident that if you are selling postcards, ancient maps, photos or similar products, you do not want them to arrive creased or distorted so will need to consider stiffeners as inserts in a close-fitting package. With glass or porcelain you will need some cushioning within a fairly rigid container. With expensive products such as antiques, you might even consider a courier service. There are, of course, specialist packers and shippers of these types of products, especially for export markets.

Where you are selling repeating-type products in significant quantities, you could consider using a fulfilment service to handle packing and delivery on your behalf. There are usually monthly charges over and above postage and packing with these companies, so you do need to be handling substantial quantities to justify the additional charges.

Upsell opportunities

Building a customer list is a vital part of this type of business. At the very least you should capture the names, addresses and email addresses of all customers and store them on a database, ideally with a record of what they have purchased. You should have leaflets about similar products you have available, either printed or computer-generated, that you can insert into delivery packages with your contact details. This type of activity frequently evokes a response that leads to additional orders. You should also send out messages to all former customers on your database from time to time, advising them about recent acquisitions that you are proposing to auction.

Ultimately you may find that if you have a large enough database, you can build a business finding and promoting products to your customers.

A full-time business

It should be clear from what I have described above that this could easily be a full-time business, although it could also be run on a small scale as a hobby business, particularly if you are knowledgeable on a particular subject. Most of your time will be spent in sourcing products, especially if you are intent on creating a range.

I have covered this subject briefly, as although it is a large and successful internet business, it is not one I have operated myself. I therefore have little experience of the levels of income that could be achieved. I have also found it necessary to treat income claims about internet businesses with a measure of scepticism. I view it as akin to the arts, where people who become well known make large incomes and even fortunes but the average performer earns very little even when constantly busy.

Internet marketing

Virtually anything can be marketed on the internet, so this is a very wide field. As an individual marketer you have the choice of selling your own products, selling other people's products under an associate or licensing agreement, or selling a wide range of products as an affiliate. Having decided how to position yourself, you then have a choice of products. Logically, however, you should restrict your range to fit a specific market – health and fitness, slimming aids and diet, golf, etc. Ideally you should have a good knowledge of the subject and an enthusiastic interest.

Study the market

There are quite literally thousands of products being sold under a variety of categories, so you need to study carefully what is already available to help identify any niche opportunities. Alternatively you can enlist as an affiliate to sell existing products on a commission basis. This is quite an attractive option, as commissions are high, usually above 50 per cent of the price realised. The reason for this is that product owners are seeking to build a list of clients to whom they can sell a range of products.

The client list

This is ultimately the most important aspect of developing an internet marketing business. It is beyond dispute that a satisfied customer will place repeat orders and will more willingly buy new products from known suppliers than unknown sources. This means that each new product promotion will evoke a higher response from existing customers than from any other given list of names. This is fundamental in the traditional mail-order businesses, where response levels are critical to financial success. With pure internet marketing, response levels are much lower, but mailing costs are negligible.

Most marketers find that many customers remain loyal for several years and will buy something every year. In such cases the list becomes the virtual goodwill of the business and can change hands for tens or even hundreds of thousands of pounds.

As an affiliate, you may capture the name but not necessarily the address, as the order is arranged by the product owner, usually through a fulfilment house.

The upsell

Acceptance of an order is also an opportunity to promote a further product at little marketing cost. This is achieved by enclosing new product literature within the delivery package, usually for a more expensive product than the initial order. Indeed, if customers order the second product, further literature can be included in the delivery package about an even more expensive additional product. This concept adds a touch of serendipity, and frequently enhances the return on each campaign.

Licences

A large business exists selling licences to would-be marketers. Here you acquire the rights to the product within the terms of the licence agreement. You may then produce or buy from a designated source and have control over the marketing and fulfilment of the product. This can be an attractive means of entry into the market, provided you are satisfied that the product you acquire has significant features you can promote. Eventually you could put together a stable of compatible products using this strategy.

Associate arrangements

Several successful internet marketers elect to expand their business by taking on 'associates' to whom they provide training and support. Arrangements vary but usually require an upfront fee in the range £1,000–£5,000, plus some form of profit-sharing agreement or royalty. In many ways this is akin to franchising. The owner usually has a number of allied products available, and others in the development stage.

Operating a website

The internet is growing so rapidly that no one website is likely to catch the attention of all potential browsers. Website style and content also influence buying decisions.

Creating a website is a job for professionals, unless you already have experience of doing so. It should not be an expensive exercise, however. The home page should identify what you are about, with supporting pages describing products. Much will depend on the nature of the product being sold, but usually it pays to offer something free on the home page, such as a report relevant to the product range. For example, if you are selling slimming aids, then a report on weight loss from an authoritative source might help you capture the names of people who visit the site and ask for the report.

This is the start of your list of prospects. They should receive an automatic friendly response thanking them for their interest, followed by the report and follow-up communications. Opinions vary about the frequency of contact, but most marketers try to send something every week – not necessarily a sales blurb. Ideally you want these contacts to keep referring to your site. This means it has to be kept fresh, with constantly changing blogs that encourage visitors to look at product literature pages and ultimately click through to order.

It can be perceived that once properly set up, this type of business is highly automated, with most things delegated. Control of the website and traffic generation then becomes the focus of the business.

Traffic generation

Internet marketing is inevitably a numbers game, and indeed, most websites have a feature that captures the number of visitors to the site, those that sign and those that eventually click through and become customers. Creating interest is therefore of paramount importance.

Most people visit browsers when searching for information. Google is widely perceived as having the dominant position, whereas in reality it accounts for less than 20 per cent of all visitors. It also charges substantially more than everybody else, whilst providing little or no information on how it ranks advertisers. However, it is widely understood that generating sales through Google is all about 'adwords'. This relates to creating a short phrase or keyword that captures the reader's interest, encouraging them to click through to your website. The essential requirement is that the adword should appear on Google's first page of product advertisers, and ideally within the first three to five names listed. Viewers are unlikely to read more than the first few headings before looking at a website to obtain more information.

The price of listing adwords varies according to the appeal of the product, but this is an area of spending that needs constant watching and analysis. It has the potential to run away with money.

Use of adwords and key phrases is an art that needs studying carefully. Much has been written about them, and several treatises on the subject are available on the web.

Most other browsers offer a far cheaper service than Google so should also be considered, and there are other forms of publicising websites. It is for most people a new concept that needs learning. There is little doubt, however, that the volume of business transacted over the internet is continuing to grow rapidly, so opportunity exists for those who study and persevere.

CHAPTER FOURTEEN

Building Your Business

Expansion can be a trap

Most of the businesses I have described are relatively easy to start, and in most cases require little market research. I have strongly advocated the use of databases, but these can be acquired for well under £5,000, including software programs.

If you buy a business, you are usually also buying a customer list and sales history. If acquiring a franchise, you generally obtain an allocated territory and marketing plans. It is only when you start a completely new product-based business that you may need to spend money finding out if a market exists. Entrepreneurs with new products have usually created or acquired them because of a known advantage in a niche or market sector. With the internet and mail order you are usually promoting something to the public and should compare your offer with your competitors to identify strengths and weaknesses.

In all these situations you should be able to launch your business without too much fear that competition will overwhelm you. As it expands, however, it is probable that competitors will start to recognise you and adapt their policies accordingly. This is less true with professional management services, but will apply with traditional professions like law and accounting, and with businesses such as estate agents and advertising agencies.

Building a knowledge base

Your first objectives with a new business are to survive and generate an income that covers your basic lifestyle expenses. Once these goals are met, usually within the first year, you need to start thinking about what you want to do next. With a business that relies on promoting your professional skills, you might reasonably decide to keep it as a one-person operation and optimise your income. In this case you would be wise to insure against health risks and try to accumulate savings for the inevitable rainy day. The moment your ambitions exceed this platform, you need to start finding out about markets, competition and limitations. I recommend you formalise this information by logging it as and when you uncover it. Cut out and retain any articles about your business sector. Set up a list of competitors, creating a computer file for each. Try to ascertain the scale of their business; consider how they operate.

You should try to quantify the market for your service in every way possible:

- Number of potential customers in your region

- Total spend

- Key competitors' share of the market

- How is the market served?

- What advantages are customers looking for?

- Why do they need the service?

- What weaknesses do you have?

- How can you overcome them?

These thoughts should be mulled over periodically; they may stimulate ideas about merging with a competitor, finding a gap in the market or introducing an innovation.

The point of vulnerability

Expansion needs handling carefully. A vast number of businesses achieve a sudden increase in sales but not profits. What is the point? It is often true that you have to increase operating costs in order to expand. Having done so, you might have the capacity to handle three times the work, so you have to plan to capture that additional work. Costs might sink you before you bring in the new business, particularly if taking on staff.

Planning is critical, and should be designed to hit clear objectives that advance the business. Consider ideas carefully; avoid acting on impulse. Think hard about cutting prices to win more business. You could be better off raising prices and turning down new, less profitable business. New commercial relationships need to be sound if you are to commit additional resources to serving them.

Employing staff

This is the first major expansion cost, so you need to be clear about why you are incurring it. In most traditional businesses it will probably be obvious: e.g. an estate agent probably wants an additional negotiator to handle more business. A market rate usually exists for such people and a major part of their income is commission-based. It is therefore relatively easy to calculate how much new business you need to justify this. An advertising agent might decide to recruit a graphic designer on the grounds that he is spending significantly more buying in the service than an employee would cost. Typically, however, you may find you simply want an extra pair of hands – a PA or secretarial assistant to manage your admin, plan meetings and keep accounting records.

Where you feel you need somebody to assist with main-line business because demand is more than you can cope with, act with care. You are making a long-term commitment that could prove expensive if you choose the wrong person. If you choose the right person who proves to be successful, you could also be breeding a competitor who might be able to steal your business from under you. In such circumstances you may find you have no legal recourse unless you have anticipated this possibility.

Write a job specification

This is relatively straightforward if your need is for a specialist such as a graphic designer. In other cases it should be based on a close analysis of the business and, indeed, your own strengths and weaknesses. Ask yourself if there is a specific function that occurs on most projects that you would like to delegate.

If we take one of the management roles with the widest market – IT consultant – we can break projects down and see that such a person needs to:

- Analyse existing systems and data produced within the business

- Determine what systems are available to simplify and/or streamline existing procedures

- Write project proposals with benefit statements

- Customise systems and instal them

- Prepare systems manuals

- Carry out staff training

You can see at a glance that a range of skills is needed and that you might be better at some than others. Some functions – such as analysis of existing systems and data collection, or writing up manuals – probably do not need a fully skilled IT consultant to perform them. They are largely clerical, with some systems knowledge. In such cases it would not be necessary to recruit a fully trained systems expert, merely an analyst at a much lower salary.

The specification would be:

Reporting to the proprietor, the systems analyst will be required to assist on client projects to:

Carry out investigations to determine how existing data is produced and used

Produce flow charts showing existing systems for agreement with clients and proprietor

Study systems proposals produced by senior consultant

Work with clients to modify existing primary records to meet needs of system changes

Assist with implementation and staff training programmes

Producing an advert

The first consideration is to determine salary ranges. This is arrived at in two ways:

- Research to assess current going rates

- Calculation as to what can be afforded

Research is relatively straightforward; current rates can be ascertained by looking at job adverts for similar personnel in local papers and technical journals and by taking advice from recruitment consultants.

For the purposes of calculation, let us assume that the consultant charges £500 per day for an average of four days per week for 45 weeks per annum. The remainder of his time is spent meeting prospective clients and on his own administration. Clearly if he is going to increase the business he will need to meet more clients. He will also need to spend time supervising and training his new assistant, and reading reports.

It is unlikely that he will be able to charge a full rate for his assistant. He might sell his time at £350 per day and achieve four and a half days per week for 45 weeks, or £70,875 increase in fees, but compensate partially by increasing his own rate to £600 per day for three and a half days per week for 45 weeks. His own saleable time would be reduced as he would have increased management and training obligations. In effect it becomes possible to increase gross income from £90,000 p.a. to a little in excess of £170,000, but that will not happen overnight.

The potential income gain is £80,000 p.a. at full capacity and if everything goes well. It rarely does, however. In my view he cannot afford to pay more than half the potential gain, inclusive of National Insurance employer's charges, and ideally around 35–40 per cent, to be safe. The salary can be increased when he reaches full capacity. In practice the position should be advertised at 'in the range £25–30,000 p.a.'. This implies a younger, less experienced person, but that probably fits the bill. The advertisement now comes together:

> Busy IT consultant requires a systems analyst to work closely with him on client projects, to carry out investigations into existing systems and to report accordingly. Thereafter the analyst will produce systems manuals and assist with implementation and staff training.
>
> Clients are based mainly in Hampshire so some travel will be necessary. The ideal candidate is unlikely to be under twenty-five years of age and will have some experience of computer systems and information flow.
>
> Salary will be in the range £25–30,000 p.a.
>
> Please apply in writing, enclosing a full CV.

The contract of employment

The appointment letter should set out the full terms of employment and be sent in duplicate, inviting the appointee to sign and return the second copy as confirmation and agreement of the terms. The letter should be on headed stationery and addressed to the new employee at his home address.

> Dear Mr Smith,
>
> Following our recent discussions, I am pleased to confirm my offer to appoint you as a systems analyst on a commencing salary of £27,000 per annum, paid monthly and with periodic review in the light of your own and the company's performance.
>
> Your duties are as set out in the attached job description, but you will be required to assist me, as proprietor, with

other work from time to time. This appointment will be for an initial probationary period of three months and thereafter will become permanent subject to written notice of termination of one month on either side. In the event of termination of this appointment, for whatever reason, it is hereby mutually agreed that you will not approach or have contact with any client of the business within one year of such termination.

You will be entitled to paid holidays that accrue at the rate of two days for each month worked up to a maximum of twenty working days per annum plus statutory holidays.

Normal hours of work are from 9 a.m. to 5.30 p.m., with one hour for lunch. You will be required to work mainly on clients' premises, as directed, but you may occasionally complete reports in your own home or in my office. You will also be required to maintain a record of time spent on work for clients and other duties as a basis for charging fees.

You will be reimbursed for travel expenses incurred on public transport in carrying out your duties or at a rate of 45p per mile up to 10,000 miles per annum and 25p per mile thereafter when using your own vehicle.

I attach a duplicate copy of this letter, which I would appreciate your signing and returning to me as confirmation of your acceptance of the terms of your appointment.

Finally I would like to welcome you to the business and trust that we will have a long and mutually satisfactory working relationship.

Yours sincerely,

Harry Jones

Director

I agree to the terms of employment as set out herein

.... Jack Smith

Dated ....

This is now a binding contract.

Acquiring property

It is widely accepted today that many businesses operate quite satisfactorily from the owner's home. This is frequently perceived as having many advantages. The first and most obvious is that it avoids or minimises overhead expenses. Parking facilities are usually better and communications easier. Nevertheless, it sometimes becomes necessary to expand, in which case additional space will be needed. The options are:

- Outright purchase

- Acquiring a lease

- Entering a licence agreement

Outright purchase

Between the end of the Second World War and about 2007 it was believed that property prices could only move in one direction. Home ownership was strongly encouraged by all governments. We lived through a long period of continuous inflation when houses could be bought with a small deposit but the gain applied to the full price, enabling buyers to make large returns on their actual deposit. Property was therefore perceived to be a safe investment.

So what has changed, and how does it affect us?

In a word, everything has changed. A housing bubble was allowed to get out of control in the first few years of this century and has not yet burst. The banks have run out of money. In fact these two things are related.

Most countries let their property bubble burst – sometimes with difficult consequences, as in Ireland and Spain – but for political reasons, the UK government has not allowed that to happen. As a result the current recession has been prolonged.

Realistically we should have taken a bigger hit and recovered faster, but politicians in a democracy are unable to handle bad news.

Traditionally building societies were rather dull but safe institutions. They allowed people to borrow up to three times the breadwinner's income and required a 10 per cent deposit. Savers placed funds in building societies and earned a modest but secure return. Modern banks, run by hot-shots who want excitement and fast returns, acquired the building societies and changed the lending criteria. Average property prices now equate to around six times the bread-winner's salary, and in places like London sometimes exceed ten times. As a consequence, a significantly large number of homeowners are using credit cards to maintain mortgage payments. This means they are borrowing at around 25 per cent per annum to service debt that costs around 5 per cent per annum, but politicians will not let banks foreclose on destitute borrowers because this would be more bad news.

It doesn't take a genius to see where this is heading, and yet the pundits are still trying to talk property prices up.

A property collapse would be a disaster for British banks, as most of their lending is to property owners rather than businesses, who are the ones actually trying to build the overall economy.

For the next few years the property market is only for specialists and gamblers. It is no place for honest managers who are trying to develop their businesses. Having said this, however, where planning situations allow, it may be worth erecting small offices in gardens or converting garages or other structures.

Leasehold property

A lease is usually for a longish term, rarely less than five years, although most have a halfway break clause. Even so, you are likely to be entering a minimum commitment of three years. This means you must be fairly certain of being able to afford the rent for this length of time. Most leases allow you to sublet, with the landlord's approval, but on terms similar to the head lease, so you have a possible escape route but probably with some hassle.

Most leases are drawn up by solicitors and often run to a hundred pages. They are designed to protect the landlord in all situations and can occasionally be onerous to tenants, who have little scope for negotiation. It is a common feature to have a redecoration, repairs and renewals clause that might oblige you to recarpet and redecorate throughout at the end of the term. This can sometimes be expensive.

Conversely, of course, a lease gives you security of tenure for the full term and usually includes an option to renew, although probably at a higher rental.

Licence agreements

These are becoming increasingly popular because of their flexibility. Typically you sign up for six months and may continue *in situ* subject to two months' notice by either party. A feature of many of these agreements is that they provide common services such as reception, telephone answering, photocopying, broadband connection, meeting rooms, etc. Many such services are charged on an as-needed basis. This is likely to be the ideal arrangement for the smaller expanding business that cannot risk immediate long-term commitments.

Conclusion

If you have arrived at this page, you are probably giving serious thought to self-employment. I do hope so, because in a changing world, there is no such thing as security. The only satisfactory alternative is self-reliance.

For many people who have enjoyed a stable, progressive career in employment, redundancy will come quite hard, but none of us can afford to live in the past and few of us can be truly confident about the future.

The UK economy is currently in a state from which it might never recover. The underlying truth is that we in the Western world have all lived too high on the hog as a consequence of easy credit terms that have enticed many of us to borrow money we cannot afford to repay.

As I write, we have a coalition government that talks about austerity and the need to cut borrowings by slashing government expenditure and raising taxes. Despite this rhetoric, the national debt is still rising and is widely forecast to double during the present government's term. It will probably reach £1.4 trillion by the time of the next election. This is almost equal to the entire annual output of the UK economy. Even worse, these figures take no account of government unfunded commitments like pensions to state employees and guarantees given under the Private Finance Initiative. They also ignore private borrowings, which are at an all-time high.

This overspending is certain to raise interest rates. A 1 per cent hike on the national debt would cost the equivalent of 3p on income tax. Interest rates could easily climb by more than 1 per cent during the next few years. Apart from the effect on the national debt, this could also have an impact on personal borrowings and force up mortgage interest rates to levels that would be unaffordable to many borrowers, despite Bank of England assurances. This would exacerbate both social and economic problems within the country.

Meantime, the emerging economies are still achieving annual growth rates that will change the balance of economic power dramatically within the next twenty years. While Europe struggles to repay its debts (and they have to be repaid, because people will stop lending to us), other countries will be building more powerful economies.

Other changes are also taking place. On the positive side, it already looks as if 'fracking' will bring about the greatest changes in the UK economy in the twenty-first century. Gas will probably replace oil. The UK has the potential to become energy-independent and also a net exporter. This will bring enormous economic benefits and hosts of new opportunities. The environmental lobby will delay this until the 2020s, but it will happen.

I do not claim to be a far-seeing visionary, but as a businessman and former operating manager, I have learned to look outwards at markets and trends within them, and to study competitors as a guide to help position individual businesses. I strongly advocate this type of thinking to those of you considering self-employment. You are in a position to turn adversity into success by joining the ranks of self-reliant people and thereby contributing to solving the national crisis.

I hope this book and some of the ideas postulated in it will help you to seize the opportunity, and that you will become successful and fulfilled by doing so.

> The UK economy is made up only of businesses. They are the country's sole source of wealth. We need more new and growing businesses.

If you do strike out on your own and feel that I can be of further help, please contact me at clive@cmadminservices.co.uk. I will be happy to respond.

Index